Toward a New Humanism

and Related Writings

Toward a New Humanism

and Related Writings

Samuel Ramos
1940

Edited and Translated, with an Introduction, by
Robert Eli Sanchez Jr.

HACKETT PUBLISHING COMPANY
INDIANAPOLIS

Copyright © 2025 by Hackett Publishing Company, Inc.

All rights reserved
Printed in the United States of America

28 27 26 25   1 2 3 4 5 6 7

For further information, please address
    Hackett Publishing Company, Inc.
    P.O. Box 44937
    Indianapolis, Indiana 46244-0937

    www.hackettpublishing.com

Cover design by Listenberger Design & Associates
Interior design by Laura Clark
Composition by Aptara, Inc.

Library of Congress Control Number: 2024950179

ISBN-13: 978-1-64792-227-6 (pbk.)
ISBN-13: 978-1-64792-228-3 (PDF ebook)
ISBN-13: 978-1-64792-229-0 (epub)

The paper used in this publication meets the minimum requirements of American National Standard for Information Sciences—Permanence of Paper for Printed Library Materials, ANSI Z39.48–1984.

∞

CONTENTS

Acknowledgments	ix
Introduction	xi
Chapter One: The Crisis of Humanism	1
Chapter Two: On the Concept of Philosophy	17
Origin of the Notion of Reality	19
Metaphysical Assumptions of Idealism	20
The Ontological Foundation of Knowledge	22
The Variation of the Categories	24
Intuition and Categories	27
Chapter Three: Theory of Objects	29
Chapter Four: Agenda for a Philosophical Anthropology	33
Axioms of Human Ontology	35
The Human Being as "Ought to Be"	38
Theories of the Human Being and the Arc of Humanism	40
A New Appraisal of Instincts	43
The Layers of the Human Being	47
Chapter Five: Objectivity of Values	51
Preliminary Remarks	51
The World of Values	55
Duty: Bridge Between the Real and the Ideal	56
Chapter Six: Moral Values	59
Chapter Seven: The Human Being as Freedom	65
Chapter Eight: Person and Personality	75
The Metaphysics of Personality	79
Personality as Duty	81
Collective Personalities	83

Chapter Nine: Conclusion	87
Related Writings	95
A Conception of Culture	95
Max Scheler	98
The Mechanization of Human Life	106
A New Humanism	111
Ortega y Gasset and Spanish America	115
The Preoccupation with Death	120
Letter to W. W. Norton & Company, Inc. by T. B. Irving	124
The "Toward" of Samuel Ramos by José Gaos	130
"Toward a New Humanism" by Eduardo Nicol	139
The Humanism of Samuel Ramos: A Guide for Contemporary Society by Rafael Moreno M.	143
Bibliography	*151*
Index	*157*

For Lydia and Mariano

ACKNOWLEDGMENTS

Translating is a thankless task. It is slow, tedious, and rarely appreciated in philosophy as an intellectual or creative achievement. It is the work done behind the scenes, typically with the anonymous contribution of many. I would like to take this opportunity, then, to acknowledge and thank those who played an essential role in bringing this volume to the light of day.

First and foremost, I would like to thank Aurelia Valero Pie, without whom there would be no translation. Early in the Pandemic, Aurelia and I began to translate Ramos's *Humanismo* together. Over several months, we met online and produced a rough first draft of the main text, line by line. The majority of our conversation was less about how to render Ramos's Spanish into compelling English prose and more about trying to make philosophical sense of particular sentences or passages, this or that transition, and in some cases, typographic errors that made certain parts almost unintelligible. We spent our time together hunting down sources and negotiating the right interpretation of ideas or arguments that were less than fully transparent in Spanish. In short, we *translated* together in the broadest sense of the term, and I am grateful that Aurelia saved me from countless mistranslations, and encouraged me to keep going.

With first draft in hand, I continued revising the translation in the classroom, mostly in response to questions, comments, and blank faces. I would like to thank Eduardo Garcia and Noah Yee Yick and the other students of Philosophy 223: Mexican Philosophy at Occidental College, as well as the students in my seminar on Mexican humanism at the University of California, Los Angeles. I am grateful for having had the opportunity to take the translation on multiple road tests.

I would like to thank members of the Mexican Philosophy Lab at the University of California San Diego, who met in November 2023 to workshop what I *thought* would be the final draft. In particular,

I would like to thank Clinton Tolley, Manuel Vargas, and Carlos Alberto Sanchez, both for their invaluable suggestions and for their friendship, encouragement, and support. A debt of gratitude is also due to Alberto Sahagún and other members of our reading group, who read drafts of the related writings at Libros Schmibros in Boyle Heights. I would also like to thank Neal Tognazzini for his invaluable support and guidance.

Special thanks are owed to the National Endowment for the Humanities, which generously granted me a Summer Stipend, enabling me to dedicate the summer of 2022 to this translation. And to Samuel Ramos Palacios for his ongoing support and willingness to grant me permission to translate his father's corpus.

Finally, I would like to thank my beautiful wife and daughter—forever my why and wherefore.

INTRODUCTION

I

Samuel Ramos Magaña was born in Zitácuaro, Michoacán, on June 8, 1897, and died in Mexico City on June 20, 1959. After spending his early years homeschooled by his father, he followed in his father's footsteps to pursue a degree in medicine at the Colegio de San Nicolás in Morelia, the capital of Michoacán. In 1917, after the sudden death of his father and one year of medical school, Ramos moved to Mexico City to enroll in the Escuela Médico Militar, a decision that would alter the course of his life and of Mexican philosophy in the twentieth century.

In Mexico City, Ramos audited courses at the Universidad Nacional Autónoma de México given by Antonio Caso, a charismatic professor of philosophy who, along with José Vasconcelos, was decisive in Ramos's decision to leave medicine and dedicate himself to philosophy. What was it that drew the young scientist to *la filosofía y letras* (philosophy and letters)? It's hard to say. However, it's clear that Ramos was drawn to Caso and Vasconcelos's call for spiritual reform in Mexico and their critique of positivism and materialism.[1] Ramos was also captivated by the belief that education reform was essential to achieving genuine emancipation after three centuries of Spanish colonialism and by the conviction that philosophy is central to education reform. In "Twenty Years of Education in Mexico" (1943), a critique of historical materialism that eulogizes Vasconcelos's tenure as Secretary of Public Education, Ramos writes: "Destiny brought a *philosopher* . . . to the great task of educating a nation."[2]

---

1. For brief introductions to the philosophies of Caso and Vasconcelos, see John H. Haddox, *Antonio Caso: Philosopher of Mexico* (Austin: University of Texas Press, 1971); and Haddox, *Vasconcelos of Mexico: Philosopher and Prophet* (Austin: University of Texas Press, 1967).

2. Samuel Ramos, "Twenty Years of Education in Mexico (1941)," in *Mexican Philosophy in the 20th Century*, ed. Carlos Alberto Sánchez and Robert Eli Sanchez Jr. (New York: Oxford University Press, 2017), 34. Emphasis added.

Ramos is remembered best for *Profile of Man and Culture in Mexico* (1934), a seminal work that defies easy classification. At the heart of the text is what Ramos refers to as a "characterology" of *lo mexicano*—that is, an interpretation of the Mexican character or the essence of Mexican identity. At the same time, the *Profile* can be read as a philosophy of Mexican history that seeks to ascertain the true "destiny" of the Mexican people. And it is the central text in Ramos's philosophy of culture, which defines culture as "a function of the spirit destined to humanize reality" and which lays out the criteria for *authentic* Mexican culture. ("By Mexican culture we mean universal culture made over into *our own*, the kind that can coexist with us and appropriately express our spirit.")[3]

The popularity of the *Profile* is due in part to its provocative thesis: that the Mexican character suffers from an inferiority complex, which explains modern Mexico's proclivity for imitating foreign ideas, models, and institutions. It is due in part to the fact that it was one of the few examples of Mexican philosophy translated into English in the twentieth century and one of the few that continue to be reprinted in Mexico. Because it was translated and published in English in 1962, it had an outsized impact on the Chicano Movement in the 1960s and the development of ethnic studies, as student activists turned to Mexican authors in an effort to diversify the curriculum and immerse themselves in texts that represented their own experiences and their desire to dismantle dominant narratives that devalued their cultural heritage.[4] The *Profile* is also cited as a paradigmatic example of the influence of José Ortega y Gasset in Latin America, the Spanish American essay, and the tensions inherent in defining Latin American cultural identity. As a result, it has achieved canonical status in Latin American philosophy. Indeed, some have argued that, although Ramos wrote widely on many topics—ranging from the visual arts, music, theater, the history of Mexican philosophy, Kant's

---

3. Samuel Ramos, *Profile of Man and Culture in Mexico*, trans. Peter G. Earle (Austin: University of Texas Press, 1962), 106–8.

4. Michael Soldatenko, "Perspectivist Chicano Studies, 1970–1985," *Ethnic Studies Review* 19, nos. 2–3 (June/October 1996): 181–208.

moral philosophy, and so on—the *Profile* is the only book by Ramos worth reading today.⁵

Despite the vast secondary literature on the *Profile* and *la filosofía de lo mexicano* (the philosophy of Mexicanness),⁶ few commentators realize that Ramos's reflections on the vices and virtues of the Mexican character, history, and culture are only part of his larger humanistic project. Nor do they fully appreciate the coherence of Ramos's philosophical project. As a result, they tend to read the *Profile* in isolation or in opposition to *Hacia un nuevo humanismo* (*Toward a New Humanism*). For instance, Patrick Romanell argues that the aims of both texts are at odds insofar as they aspire to competing ideals of being human:

> The dilemma in Ramos the neo-humanistic nationalist of Mexico originates from his whole effort to do equal justice to two ideals of man which, as postulated in the author's particular scheme of thought, are individually attractive but mutually exclusive: The neo-Orteguian localized ideal of *Mexican man* in the concrete (*Profile*, pp. 97–98, 154–156), on the one hand, and the neo-humanistic universalized

---

5. Guillermo Hurtado, "Samuel Ramos, filósofo," *Cuadernos Americanos* 139, no. 1 (2012): 59–69. At the end of the introductory paragraph, Hurtado asks, "Is it right that everything Ramos wrote [other than the *Profile*] has been all but forgotten?" After his overview of Ramos's philosophy, he responds, "My answer is that readers' sentence of silence is not wrong: [the *Profile*] is Ramos's most important book and will certainly continue to be read by future generations. The rest of his corpus has lost its force and is covered in patina" (68). Hurtado has since changed his view concerning Ramos's larger corpus. See fn. 17. However, that *lo mexicano* is Ramos's primary theme, and that his best-known work, *El perfil del hombre y la cultura en México*, is the primary text in this tradition, is by far the standard view. See, for example, Elsa Cecilia Frost's succinct but insightful effort to rescue the "theme of Samuel Ramos," which she argues is the leitmotif of Mexican thought despite its being eclipsed by the prevailing fervor for analytic philosophy. "El tema de Samuel Ramos," *Diálogos: Artes, Letras, Ciencias humanas* 15, no. 6 (noviembre–diciembre, 1979): 46–47.

6. For an introduction to *la filosofía de lo mexicano*, see Emilio Uranga, *Analysis of Mexican Being*, trans. Carlos Alberto Sánchez (London: Bloomsbury Academic, 2021): 93–101; and Abelardo Villegas, *La filosofía de lo mexicano* (México: Fondo de Cultura Económica, 1960).

ideal of *the complete man* as such (*Hacia*, pp. 72, 54). Either idea of man may be defended separately (in theory at least) without clashing with the other, but not both at the same time, except by completely compromising the issue eclectically, as Ramos tried desperately in the end to avoid an unavoidable choice confronting him squarely as pioneer defender of the nationalization of the Mexican mind.[7]

The thesis underwriting Romanell's criticism is that the *Profile* is deeply influenced by the perspectivism of Ortega y Gasset, and that Ramos's later work is more universal in scope.[8] However, it is worth noting that Ramos does not mention Ortega y Gasset once in the first two editions of the *Profile* (1934, 1938), nor is there evidence that he was developing a neo-Orteguian position in the years leading up to the *Profile*. By contrast, Ramos does discuss his neo-humanistic ideal in the *Profile*, even referring to it as the "conclusion" of the book (see "A New Humanism"); he does cite well-known humanists, such as Max Scheler and Robert Curtius; and he did write at length about humanism before 1934 (see, for example, "Max Scheler" and "A Conception of Culture").

To be fair, Ramos is largely to blame for this misleading interpretation of the *Profile*. In "The History of Philosophy in Mexico" (1943), he took the opportunity to place himself at the center of the philosophy of culture in Mexico, stating that it was Ortega y Gasset who provided the generation of philosophers emerging between 1925 and 1930—that is, Ramos—the "epistemological justification for a national philosophy."[9] (See also "Ortega y Gasset and Spanish

---

7. Patrick Romanell, "Samuel Ramos on the Philosophy of Mexican Culture: Ortega and Unamuno in Mexico," *Latin American Research Review* 10, no. 3 (Autumn 1975): 101.

8. This assumption is widespread. It is the view held, for example, by Soldatenko in his essay on Chicano Studies, and by Carlos Alberto Sánchez, who writes, "In this sense, Ramos's philosophy is indeed Ortegean." "From Ortega y Gasset to Mexican Existentialism: Toward a Philosophical Conception of Chicano Identity," *Southwest Philosophical Studies* 25, no. 1 (2003): 55.

9. Samuel Ramos, "The History of Philosophy in Mexico (1943)," in *Mexican Philosophy in the 20th Century: Essential Readings*, ed. Carlos Alberto Sánchez and Robert Eli Sanchez Jr. (New York: Oxford University Press, 2017): 68.

America.") Ramos also added six chapters to the third edition of the *Profile*, which had the effect of concealing the fact that its original concluding chapter, "The Profile of Man," is a call for humanism. In short, because *la filosofía de lo mexicano*—not humanism—became the dominant theme for the following generation of philosophers and intellectuals in Mexico, Ramos was willing to foreground his own interpretation of the Mexican character at the risk of downplaying the broader complexity and coherence of his thought.

Far from scholarly squabbling over chronology and references, the insistence that the *Profile* is one chapter in Ramos's neo-humanistic project promises a fresh take on Ramos's thought and contribution to Mexican philosophy, and on the meaning and value of Mexican philosophy in a "post-Western world."[10] For one thing, the question concerning the distinctive value of Mexican philosophy, and of comparative philosophy more generally, hinges on whether we can resolve Ramos's dilemma as Romanell articulates it. And while Ortega y Gasset's perspectivism provides one solution, it is not the only solution, a complete solution, or the basis of Ramos's solution. Instead, Scheler and Nicolai Hartmann exerted at least as much influence on Ramos's belief that the dilemma could be resolved, particularly Scheler's conceptions of *culture*, *personality*, and *humanism*.

One might be tempted to argue, as Romanell's criticism suggests, that the *Profile* and *Toward a New Humanism* represent two separate stages in the development of Ramos's thought—that we might speak of a first Ramos (the neo-Orteguian) and a second Ramos (the

---

See also Robert Eli Sanchez Jr., "The Philosophy of Mexican Culture," in *Latin American and Latinx Philosophy: A Collaborative Introduction*, ed. Robert Eli Sanchez Jr. (New York: Routledge, 2020), 100–119.

10. This phrase was coined by Carlos Alberto Sánchez to describe the ambiguous relationship Mexican philosophy has to the Western tradition. "My claim is that Mexican philosophy is *not Western* in the sense of being but a branch of the Western philosophical tree, but also that it is *not non-Western* in the sense that it can be considered part of the 'non-Western' philosophical tradition (like Indian or Chinese philosophy)." Instead, Mexican philosophy has appropriated the Western tradition and made it its own, but only to critique it from within and go beyond it. *Mexican Philosophy for the 21st Century: Relajo, Zozobra, and Other Frameworks for Understanding Our World* (London: Bloomsbury Academic, 2023), 4.

neo-humanist). However, we find Ramos's neo-humanistic universalized ideal all over the *Profile*. Consider one example. Chapter 8 of *Toward a New Humanism* develops an account of "person" or "personality," a quasi-technical term that denotes one's "true self," whose "mission . . . is to keep the human spirit from coming to a halt." In the *Profile*, Ramos writes: "Just as it should turn away from a universalist type of culture without roots in Mexico, our capital city should reject all picturesque Mexicanism lacking in universality. The ideal yet to be achieved, we might say, is *personality* subjected to a formula which could harmonize the specific values. . . . The time has come for Mexico to bring forth the fruits of its *personality*" (*Profile* 112, emphasis added). Here Ramos is not using *personality* in the sense of *character*, as in, the behavior that distinguishes one's personality from different personality types. Everyone has their own personality or character in this sense, but the sense in which Ramos is using the term (i.e., "a general phenomenon in which human spirituality is projected") is the highest degree of spirituality "reached only by a few individuals." Compare this further to Ramos's use of the term in "Max Scheler" (1928): "How well [Scheler's theory of the person] explains certain historical phenomena in Spanish America! Why do our cultural ventures almost always produce such mediocre results? Because the instruments at our disposal are, exclusively, *works* of culture; our scarcity of cultured *persons* is alarming. Herein lies, for example, the problem of higher education that, for us, is a problem of persons."

By focusing on the continuity of Ramos's thought, we will find that the aims of the *Profile* and *Toward a New Humanism* are indeed complementary, as Rafael Moreno asserts in "The Humanism of Samuel Ramos: A Guide for Contemporary Society," and that they ought to be read together as reciprocal texts: "The 1934 text anticipates and introduces the one published in 1940, and the latter supplies the theory that transforms the former into a fully philosophical text. . . . In fact, today the various essays that constitute the *Profile* can be read as a final chapter of *Toward a New Humanism*, or conversely, *Toward a New Humanism* can be read as the theoretical culmination of Ramos's meditations on Mexico." Moreover, by reading these two texts together, we may also find that there is a more compelling answer to the problem of comparative philosophy lurking in the eclectic cast of characters—in addition to, or possibly in spite of, Ortega y Gasset—that Ramos brings into dialogue throughout his corpus.[11]

II

Toward a New Humanism was in part a response to the crisis consuming Europe in 1940. On one level, the "crisis of humanism" was—and is—practical, urgent, and familiar. For Ramos, civilization had become an "instrument of death" and humanity found itself in the paradoxical situation of having to defend itself against its own creations. Likewise, today, we are threatened by addiction to our devices, nuclear annihilation, biochemical and cyber warfare, self-driving cars, runaway artificial intelligence, global warming, and environmental collapse. In an image, we are not unlike the Little Tramp in *Modern Times* (1936), who is knocked about by an eating machine that we are led to believe eventually leaves him hungry.

On a deeper level, however, Ramos lamented the "internal contradiction" that splits modern consciousness into opposing stances toward life—one that views the universe as a giant machine (or computer) and seeks to dominate nature, and the other that views the universe as a reflection of the human subject. What makes these two

---

11. "The problem of comparative philosophy" might also be referred to as "the problem of truth," as Abelardo Villegas describes it. Roughly, what I am referring to is the problem of reconciling the effort to define what is distinctive and original about a particular philosophical tradition, such as Mexican or Chinese philosophy, and the effort to preserve what is universal and objective about philosophical truth. In the case of Mexican philosophy, the *Profile* and Ortega y Gasset's perspectivism represent the heart of the problem, and Villegas finds their solution inadequate. By applying a wider lens and looking at Ramos's interpretation of *lo mexicano* in view of his new humanism, as well as comparing combining Ortega y Gasset's perspectivism with Scheler's humanism and Scheler's and Hartmann's formal ethics, we may inch closer to justifying a "philosophy *of lo mexicano*" and distinctive philosophical traditions more generally. Abelardo Villegas, "The Problem of Truth (1960)," in *Mexican Philosophy in the 20th Century: Essential Readings*, ed. Carlos Alberto Sánchez and Robert Eli Sanchez Jr. (New York: Oxford University Press, 2017), 245–59.

conceptions of the universe "contradictory," on Ramos's account, is that the modern mind has turned them into competing "ways of valuing life." In other words, the practical crisis of humanism is fundamentally a crisis of values. The modern mind is *torn* between the material and the spiritual and feels the need to choose between them, typically leading to one-sided worldviews—that is, one that privileges the material side of life (e.g., naturalism, mechanism, positivism, materialism, "bourgeois psychology") or the spiritual side of life (e.g., spiritualism, idealism, asceticism) at the expense of the other. Further, because the material dimension of life (what Ramos calls "civilization") has all but extinguished the spiritual side of life (what he calls "culture") in the Western world, we confuse the means for the ends, failing to realize that the development of technology, technique, and method—which, over time, has become an end itself—is ultimately meant to serve authentically human values. What we lack, in other words, is an objective table of values to guide or orient science and technology, which, for Ramos, are "lower" on the scale of values.[12]

The thesis underwriting *Toward a New Humanism* is that "the exterior events of life reflect the idea of what it means to be human, the consciousness or unconsciousness of our true destiny.... The thesis of this book was inspired by the eternal validity of the Socratic maxim, which says unto us: know thyself." In part, Ramos is rejecting historical materialism as the best explanation of the origin of the crisis. "Today humanism emerges as an ideal to combat the sub-humanity brought about by bourgeois capitalism and materialism." In part, his goal is to demonstrate the relevance of philosophy in a time of crisis. On Ramos's historical analysis, the origin of the crisis is Cartesian

---

12. It is useful to compare *Toward a New Humanism* to other critiques of the modern age and modern philosophy, particularly the rapid accumulation of knowledge, the hazards of dualism, and the unimpeded march of technological and technical advance. See, for example, Søren Kierkegaard's *The Present Age*, Walter Benjamin's *The Work of Art in the Age of Mechanical Reproduction*, Oswald Spengler's *Man and Technics*, and William Barrett's *Death of the Soul: From Descartes to the Computer* and *The Illusion of Technique: A Search for Meaning in a Technological Civilization*.

dualism and the philosophical inclination to reduce the diversity of phenomena to a unity so that the clash between culture and civilization is ultimately rooted in the conception of the human being as composed of two irreconcilable elements: *res cogitans* and *res extensa*. In other words, because Descartes and subsequent philosophers were unable to solve the problem of psycho-physical parallelism and the problem of other minds—an artificial problem that *they* created—and given the unprecedented developments in science, technology, exploration, global finance, and colonialism, the modern mind has drifted away from the spiritual and toward a unilateral conception of life that favors technical civilization. What is missing is a comprehensive conception of the human being, and consequently of the universe, as a *totality*.

To produce a conception of the integral human being, one that does not reduce the psychological to the physical or instinctive, is the aim of philosophical anthropology, the heart of the book.[13] The fundamental task of philosophical anthropology is to analyze what is essential in what we think the human being is and ought to be. Its guiding assumption is that human existence is an irreducible object that merits its own science, and that the objects of the other sciences converge in the human being. In this way, philosophical anthropology is prior to the other sciences, or as Ramos puts it:

> Anthropology, then, is not a synthesis of knowledge taken from different sciences, but an independent field of knowledge that corresponds directly to its object and that, with the ideas it obtains, should provide the other sciences guidance concerning their bodies of knowledge. This is to say that philosophical anthropology is a fundamental

---

13. The current translation is largely based on the second edition of the text, although I worked with all editions to produce this translation. The first and third editions of the book were titled *Hacia un nuevo humanismo: Programa de una antropología filosófica* (Toward a New Humanism: Agenda for a Philosophical Anthropology). It is not clear why Ramos, or the editors, abandoned the subtitle in the second edition and in Ramos's *Obras Completas*. I have chosen to leave out the subtitle so as not to conjure misleading associations with the history of philosophical anthropology since. Other discrepancies among the editions are minor or non-existent, as far as I could tell.

and basic science, and that the conclusions of the sciences that study partial aspects of human beings ought to be interpreted through its principles. Since the other sciences existed before, once anthropology determines its fundamental principles, scientific theories that have developed without any guiding conception of the human must be revised.

Another distinguishing feature of philosophical anthropology is that given that the human being is an axiological entity—one axiom of anthropology that asserts that to be human is essentially to be guided by values—it is a normative discipline that considers the human being a "citizen of two worlds" and a mediator between the real and ideal. But anthropology does not, however, resort to idealism, which Ramos considers a form of subjectivism and a one-sided or incomplete view of the human being and universe.

The chapters of *Toward a New Humanism* organize the contemporary philosophical theories that point in the direction of a new humanism. What makes Ramos's humanism "new" is its trajectory (see "A New Humanism"). If Renaissance humanism sought to achieve what is humanly possible through a secular effort to locate human potential in *this* world, Ramos's neo-humanism swings in the other direction: it seeks to elevate human dignity to something "higher" than the various forms of materialism that dominate modern intellectual life, again without resorting to a form of spiritualism that disparages the physical dimension of life in favor of the spirit. He writes, "Simply put, we might say that whereas classical Humanism was a movement downward from above, the new Humanism ought to appear as a movement in exactly the opposite direction, that is, upward from below."

Aside from the introductory and concluding chapters, which provide an overview of the crisis, the middle chapters organize the various philosophical theories thematically and might be read as responding to a series of potential objections or questions. In response to the potential worry that by placing the human being at the center of the cosmos we risk sliding into subjectivism, Ramos affirms realism over idealism (chapter 2). Indeed, the text as a whole can be read as a critique of idealism in the spirit of Ortega y Gasset.[14] In response to the view that all phenomena can be unified and measured for the sake of scientific explanation, Ramos proposes a new "theory of objects" and Husserl's "regional ontology" (chapter 3) to develop the view that the universe is pluralistic. In response to the naturalist's tendency to reduce human consciousness to instinct, Ramos defends the autonomy of conscious life by presenting a new "appraisal of instincts," Ortega y Gasset's division of the human being into vitality, soul, and spirit, and Scheler's concept of the *person* (chapter 4). Chapters 5–7 defend the objectivity of values, of moral values in particular, and of freedom. Indeed, not unlike William Barrett's *The Illusion of Technique*, the whole text can be read as a defense of human freedom.

One potential criticism of the content and structure of the text is that Ramos merely summarizes the views of others and does not introduce an original or systematic theory of his own. Ramos himself anticipates this criticism when he writes:

> The ideas presented in this book are a summary of the author's philosophical convictions. The exposition was born from a kind of

---

14. As with all of his philosophy, Ortega y Gasset's crusade against idealism is nuanced. José Sánchez Villaseñor captures the tenor of Ortega y Gasset's critique well when he writes: "To Ortega, Kant was an introvert who refused to face reality. He was diffident and suspicious, concerned not with knowing but with knowing that he knew. His philosophical reflection confined him to the field of the epistemological. This frame of mind was due, in Ortega's opinion, to the fact that while ancient philosophy flowered from confidence and was born of warriors, modern philosophy, child of suspicion and caution, was born of the bourgeoisie. The decisive factor for understanding Kant is his German background. The German soul suffers from metaphysical isolation, from congenital introversion. The man of the South is a man of the streets open to a thousand allurements from reality. Hence, the soul of the South tends to build its philosophy on the exterior world." *Ortega y Gasset, Existentialist: A Critical Study of His Thought and Its Sources*, trans. Joseph Small, S. J. (Chicago: Henry Regnery Company, 1949), 47–48. The reader may compare this description of Ortega y Gasset to Juan Hernández Luna's *Samuel Ramos: Su filosofar sobre lo mexicano*, given that the thesis underwriting Hernández Luna's intellectual biography of Ramos is that Ramos's philosophizing about *lo mexicano* is the product of his psychological extroversion and turn toward reality.

self-examination, a liquidation of ideas, undertaken in order to participate in a philosophical debate taking place in the contemporary world.... The aim of these chapters is not to produce a philosophical treatise that presents its problems systematically. They should be read only as a selection of philosophical ideas arranged according to a personal perspective. I believe that all philosophical questions flow from one central problem that is more or less the focus of speculative interest: the human being and our world.

However, the reader should bear in mind that one feature of Ramos's neo-humanism, both in the *Profile* and in *Toward a New Humanism*, is to defend an alternative way of thinking about originality (see "The Humanism of Samuel Ramos: A Guide for Contemporary Society"). Ramos writes: "Philosophy subsists not only on the creation of original ideas, but also on the more modest act of rethinking what has already been thought, on the mental reproduction of the entire process of philosophical speculation that, in a way, is a recreation of philosophy. This is the only method that leads to the world of philosophy and to unlocking its secrets." Originality consists in the act of *rethinking*, which is to say, in the act of assimilating thoughts that are already available or making them *one's own*. This is also how he defines authentic Mexican culture in the *Profile*: "By Mexican culture we mean universal culture made over into *our own*, the kind that can coexist with us and appropriately express our spirit" (*Profile*, 108).[15]

---

15. Compare this view of originality to what Ramos says about the eighteenth-century philosopher Benito Díaz de Gamarra: "From this point of view, it is clear that there is not in the entire history of [Mexican] thought a single philosopher who can be considered original or creative. To this day, we cannot boast of having contributed to a great philosophical view to universal culture.... Philosophy is a particular function of the spirit that reaches its full potential in itself, even if it only reproduces the thought process that in the great philosophers led to the creation of new ideas. Gamarra is not an imitator of modern philosophers; he is a mind that has assimilated the content of their philosophy, on his own, after examining and selecting what seemed true in the light of his rational consciousness. There is another criterion for evaluating Hispanic-American philosophical production, which is to ascertain whether a work, more than being original in the strict sense of the term, has been assimilated to our American existence and influences the organization of our culture. It seems to me that the most

In any case, for José Gaos, Ramos is not necessarily the best reader of his own text. In "The 'Toward' of Samuel Ramos," Gaos claims that Ramos does provide "a systemization of the history of contemporary philosophy, or, what amounts to the same, a system of the history of contemporary philosophy." And he suggests that his choice of which ideas and theories to include, and not to include, presents an original way of viewing the world. (Or as Ramos puts it: "The nuances of personality are revealed, above all, in the things the individual chooses and leaves out to form a world of one's own.") Again, it is the act of making the thoughts of others one's own, which is why Gaos claims, "The event that is Ramos's book consists, in sum, in the decisive role it plays in helping to achieve the assimilation of contemporary philosophy for Mexico." Again, to assimilate is not to imitate; it is to make an existing idea, argument, or theory one's *own*, which is an achievement in itself, and something one may fail to do. This is why Gaos warns: "Mexican thought is at a critical juncture and must not get in the way of its *own* thinking"—that is, must not get in the way of becoming itself, becoming Mexican, through its philosophical thinking or rethinking.

What makes Ramos's thought "post-Western," in part, is that, like other Mexican philosophers at the time, Ramos imagined that "the future is ours." That is, writing between two world wars, with European civilization on the brink of collapse, Ramos and others took seriously the belief that a new humanism would emerge in America,[16] and that humanism and a higher sense of values

---

eminent value that a philosophical work can have for us lies in the effectiveness of somehow awakening an awareness of our own being, in helping us to define the formation of our character." "The History of Philosophy in Mexico (1943)," 66–67.

16. It is worth noting that Latin Americans also refer to themselves as "Americans" or *Americanos*—that is, someone from "the Americas." To say that the future lies in America, then, is not to say that it lies in the United States. Indeed, Ramos warns that the mechanization of life that was leading to the self-destruction of Europe was already prevalent in the United States and was encroaching on the Americas south of the US–Mexico border. There is also a provincialism lurking behind our use of "American," precisely the kind of provincialism that Ramos's

were—are—needed to resist the threat of narrow-minded nationalism and authoritarianism, the colossus of modern technology, particularly weapons of mass destruction that are increasingly more sophisticated, powerful, and autonomous, and the "abandonment of culture" (i.e., the title of chapter 6 of the *Profile*). As Guillermo Hurtado describes the Mexican intellectual climate of the time:

> Even though the old continent wasn't completely reduced to ashes, postwar civilization had to be founded upon other bases, separated from the barbarism demonstrated by the Europeans in their criminal use of technology, their utter disregard for human life, and their violation of everything of value. This was perhaps the first time that Mexicans considered their responsibility in the face of the circumstances all of humanity found itself. The new humanism, as Samuel Ramos called it, had to be formulated in America, from the American experience, a humanism that is caring, compassionate, fraternal, and above all, peace-loving.[17]

Unfortunately, we have yet to learn our lesson: World War III is not unimaginable; we continue to privilege science and technology above, and often at the expense of, the arts and humanities; we are even more disoriented by the insanely rapid accumulation of knowledge and access to information; and anxiety and depression have become

---

new humanism and Mexican philosophy sought to combat. Edgar Sheffield Brightman expresses the point this way: "As José Vasconcelos has dreamed of a cosmic race, so Mexican philosophy has aspired to cosmic truth. This book brings home to its readers the values and the limitations of provincialism in thought, while mirroring at the same time the essential struggle of all philosophy to overcome provincialism. Provincialism! How difficult it is for us North Americans to eradicate from our own attitudes. Our country is 'God's Country.' We arrogate to ourselves the very name of 'American,' which by right belongs to every citizen of North, Central, and South America. We call our country '*The* United States,' in sublime disregard of the Mexican United States as well as the United States of Venezuela." "Forward," in *Making of the Mexican Mind: A Study in Recent Mexican Thought* (Lincoln: University of Nebraska Press, 1952), 4–5.

17. Guillermo Hurtado, "El pensamiento ante la guerra mundial," *La Razón de México*, March 30, 2024, https://www.razon.com.mx/opinion/columnas/guillermo-hurtado/pensamiento-mexicano-guerra-mundial-570993.

permanent fixtures of modern life. In short, we find ourselves ever deeper in a crisis of humanism.

III

The related writings in this volume serve a number of purposes. The first six by Ramos are meant to convey the development and coherence of Ramos's thought from 1925 on and to illustrate the continuity between the *Profile* and *Toward a New Humanism*. They also serve to demonstrate that, although Ramos mentions Mexico only once in *Toward a New Humanism*, Mexico was undoubtedly on his mind as he developed the ideas that resulted in the 1940 text. In other words, they serve to help the reader identify the tacit references and allusions to Mexico hidden throughout *Toward a New Humanism*, and thus serve to help the reader respond to critics who claim that there is nothing Mexican about humanism in Mexico.[18] "The Conception of Culture" and "Max Scheler" point the reader in the direction of Scheler's species of phenomenology, philosophical anthropology, personalism, philosophical anthropology, and humanism, and suggest that, along with the philosophy of Nicolai Hartmann, Scheler is perhaps the dominant influence on Ramos's thought, more so than Ortega y Gasset. "A New Humanism" and "The Mechanization of Life" serve as reminders of the historical context in which Ramos was writing—between two world wars and the rise of fascism—because

---

18. One such critic is O. A. Kubitz, who writes, "Ramos believes that [despite the claims of historical materialism and irrationalism to the contrary, philosophy is relevant in a time of crisis], and he substantiates this claim by offering what may be called a general hypothesis of regions of being in all of which man participates. But the very generality of the hypothesis seems to be the source of criticism. It is an approach to all types of human situations. Hence, if it is desirable that Mexican humanism should have its own unique character, Ramos' approach cannot of itself and without further investigation provide the concrete details of a practical program for a specifically Mexican humanism." "Humanism in Mexico," *Philosophy and Phenomenological Research* 2, no. 2 (December 1941): 217–18. The related writings are meant to serve the reader in conducting just such further investigation.

although allusions to the wars in the text are few and far between, Ramos's call for a new humanism, especially in Mexico, is a direct response to the events unfolding in Europe and to the political dimension of the crisis in humanism. "The Preoccupation with Death" might seem out of place since, at least on the surface, there is no mention of humanism. However, on closer inspection, the reader may find that Ramos's explanation of our contemporary obsession with death is the product of the same "internal contradiction" discussed in *Toward a New Humanism*, that is, the artificial opposition modern philosophy has created between the value of the life of the body and the value of the life of the soul, as well as the rise of individualism (and the decline of personalism).

The remaining four writings provide synoptic overviews of the content of the text and, in addition to the other reviews already available in English, are included to help orient the reader. There are, of course, many more reviews in Spanish that one might consult, but these four are included because they each shine a different and suggestive light on the text. T. B. Irving's letter to W. W. Norton & Co., essentially a book proposal, suggests that this translation is long overdue and that Alfonso Reyes, perhaps *the* authority on Mexican letters at the time, thought that Ramos's text might best represent Mexican thought to the North American reading public. José Gaos's "The 'Toward' of Samuel Ramos" provides a brief historical introduction to "contemporary philosophy," which he claims Ramos organizes thematically, and Gaos introduces the question of the "Mexicanicity" of the text and the value of the text for Mexicans. "Toward a New Humanism," aside from providing a helpful summary, highlights an aspect of Ramos's writing and philosophy that not only will help the reader to appreciate certain idiosyncrasies of the text but also discusses one of the great virtues of Ramos's larger corpus, including *Toward a New Humanism*: "In this way, Samuel Ramos is like a protagonist of the ideas that he expounds; his personality is present not only in the position he takes toward them, but even in the spirit governing the logical task of systematically organizing and articulating its themes." And perhaps more than anyone, Rafael Moreno writes best about the overarching theme of Ramos's thought, convincing at least this reader that we are mistaken for reading either the *Profile* or *Toward a New Humanism* without the other.

Robert Eli Sanchez Jr.
Occidental College, Los Angeles
January 2025

CHAPTER ONE

The Crisis of Humanism

Modern consciousness is characterized by a deep dualism in our way of valuing life, which divides it into two isolated regions: the spiritual and the material. The individual is faced with a choice whose only solution is to opt for one of the two conflicting values. This dualist mentality attempts to ground itself in the very constitution of reality, which everywhere appears divided according to the characteristics of spirit and matter. The majority of educated people accept dualism as an indisputable fact and act accordingly, orienting their lives to one side or the other, depending on which value they prefer. It is inevitable, then, that whichever is chosen, one aspect of life is sacrificed, and even though everyone is convinced that there's nothing to be done, this sacrifice tears us in two and our lives pass by in the throes of deep uneasiness and discontent.

The root of dualism appears to lie deep in the being of the human, which is split into tendencies that pull in opposite directions, either toward the satisfaction of the soul or of the body. Because these tendencies have been at work over the course of a long historical process, they have created a world in which the bifurcation of the human is manifest in things and is defined, so to speak, in macroscopic terms. Dualism finds multiple expressions across the various fields of human life, such as the social, political, and economic organization of almost every nation, as well as the ideologies that compete to win the favor of the majority. Here we will consider one of the most important aspects of dualism, namely the clash between civilization and culture.[1]

---

1. [Ramos is alluding to a discussion that began in the second half of the nineteenth century, involving thinkers like Friedrich Nietzsche, Oswald Spengler, Paul Valéry, and Bertrand Russell. In the Spanish-speaking world, the main reference is Miguel de Unamuno's 1896 essay, "Civilización y cultura," in *Obras*

1

The backbone of modern culture is the spiritual sense of life, whose origin dates back to the two most powerful influences on European history: Greek thought and Christianity. At the dawn of our age, upon finding a rational justification in modern metaphysics, this sense of life grew independent and assumed new forms befitting the times. At the same time, as our knowledge of nature advanced and opened practical possibilities hitherto undreamed of, we discovered the material side of life, whose magnitude and importance were slowly revealed. In a word, the development of natural science transformed and amplified the concept of the universe and gave us a powerful instrument to dominate material forces. The expansion of knowledge likewise increased human potential, which built a material civilization in grand dimensions never before seen. The nerve centers of this new organism are modern cities which thrive on industry and commerce. This urban setting awakened and spread everywhere the material interests of the human being, whose personality aligned with the demands of their environment through mimesis, not unlike how an animal takes on the color of nearby objects. Instinctive life, representing the natural within us, became aware of its rights and imposed itself on the spirit with an air of vengeance in opposition to the humiliating servitude it had endured for so long.

A new kind of human being emerged, proud and dominant, full of contempt for ancient morality and eager to expand the life of the body, employing the goods civilization had to offer. The enjoyment of wealth as an instrument of power and means for achieving material well-being and a comfortable life; the pleasures of sex, sport, travel, mobility, and other exciting diversions; all these constitute the multifaceted perspective through which the existence of the modern human was projected. This type of human is best represented by the bourgeoisie whose psychology, as [Werner] Sombart has described with penetrating clarity, combines traits characterized by an attraction

---

Selectas (Madrid: Biblioteca Nueva, 1986), 153–59. All notes, or parts of notes, enclosed in square brackets are the translator's.]

to material values.[2] Civilization is driven by materialism and develops along a different path from that of culture, but together they create a dramatic tension whose painful effects are felt in the minds of many modern humans.

Descartes offered the first philosophical justification of dualism early in the seventeenth century. In opposition to the Scholastic worldview, and employing a strictly rationalist method, this thinker conceived of the universe as a vast machine.[3] Carving his own path, the philosopher arrived at the same conclusion as his contemporary Galileo: "Nature is written in the language of mathematics."[4] The universe was subjected to a process of simplification for the sake of explaining all of it easily under the light of reason and by means of clear and distinct ideas. The immense qualitative variety of things was transformed into a uniform order of magnitudes—colors were reduced to the frequencies of vibrations, for example—in a way that suggested at the start that all natural phenomena can be measured. Armed with this methodological hypothesis, the philosopher needed only two explanatory principles to reconstruct the totality of existence in one grand system: matter and movement. Descartes did not stop when he reached the organic world but applied with implacable rigor the same mechanistic explanation to living beings, which he also considered machines. With this daring affirmation, Descartes abruptly turned his back on the old doctrine of Aristotle, untouched for centuries, which described life as a final cause. In the modern system, there was no room for any such cause.

Descartes persisted and logically arrived at the conclusion that the human being is part of the mechanistic order. If we are a corporeal entity, we must of necessity be machines. But here, in the human being, is where the dualism behind Descartes's thought bursts in:

---

2. [Werner Sombart, *Der Bourgeois: Zur Geistesgeschichte des modernen Wirtschaftsmenschen* (Munich and Leipzig: Duncker & Hublot, 1913). English translation: *The Quintessence of Capitalism: The Study of the History and Psychology of the Modern Business Man*, trans. M. Epstein (New York: E. P. Dutton and Company, 1915).]
3. [René Descartes, "Treatise on Man," in *The World and Other Writings* (Cambridge: Cambridge University Press, 1998), 97–169.]
4. [In Galileo Galilei, *The Assayer* (1623).]

unlike the animal, which is a machine pure and simple, the human is a thinking machine. It is simply a fact that thought, which lacks extension, cannot be considered a material substance. Thought belongs to a distinct ontological category that, without hesitating, Descartes placed in the realm of the spirit. Human nature, then, turns out to be composed of two elements: the thinking substance (spirit) and the extended substance (matter). Having established this deep separation between the two constitutive principles of being human, philosophy faced a new metaphysical problem: how to explain psycho-physiological parallelism. How do the actions of the soul align with those of the body?

Descartes maintained that the interaction between bodies can only be explained by mechanical causes. Collision is the only means by which one body has influence over another. So, if the soul is incorporeal, how can it physically act upon the body and *vice versa*? Here we have a problem that, having postulated the radical duality of substances, cannot be resolved by reason. Employing an arbitrary and fantastical theory, Descartes believed that he had untied the knot: the soul inserts itself into the body through the pineal gland. The three great philosophers following Descartes who were troubled by the same puzzle—Malebranche, Spinoza, and Leibniz—also wasted their time trying to solve it by means of solutions increasingly more artificial. Could it be that in the end there is no real difficulty and that Descartes manufactured the problem? Be that as it may, we can say that the historical development of the human being after Descartes seemed to fully confirm his theory of dualism. The spiritual and the material have become two isolated worlds that have little or no contact. Above all, dualism is represented in civilization and culture, which make tangible the internal division of the human being. At a certain point in its development, civilization gained a momentum of its own, which we have been unable to impede, increasingly emphasizing our mechanical character.

Mechanism [*el maquinismo*],[5] designed to make human work easier, soon became an instrument of servitude. We squandered a great opportunity to liberate ourselves from physical labor and to replace human slavery with the machine. Today our admiration for power has made us into faithful servants of the machine, which, for many of us, has risen to the level of a new fetish. The enormously tempting power of the machine tends to impose a mechanistic order on society, and through a kind of mimetism, the individual is also mechanized. In this way, time seems to have affirmed the Cartesian view that, in the eighteenth century, drove the committed materialist, [Julien Offray de] La Mettrie, to write a book titled *Man the Machine* [*L'homme machine*].

A psychoanalytic theory of history would interpret this phenomenon [i.e., mechanism] as revenge against the long oppression that the spirit imposed upon human beings. A misunderstanding as one-sided as that of materialism, the spiritualist sense of life overlooks the values of concrete reality. Plato, the first advocate of spiritualism, thought of the body as "the prison of the soul," and this misunderstanding of the body leads to the ascetic ideal that consistently accompanies the spiritual sense of life, even in modern culture. Eventually, the ascetic's systematic negation of the vital values led the instincts to rebel and, drunk with triumph, to drag the defeated spirit through the mud.

Materialism and positivism, specifically the view that conceives of the human as an entirely "natural" being, further justified, philosophically, the rebellion of the instincts. The higher functions of the soul, such as intelligence, the will, and feeling, were thought of merely as an extension of the instincts, destined to serve them indirectly. Given this view, the human was reduced only to the instinctive, implying that we belong to the order of animality. The only thing that

---

5. ["Machinism" is a closer translation of *el maquinismo*. It refers generally to the use of machines in lieu of human labor. In the nineteenth century, it was considered dangerous for the reasons outlined in this paragraph. However, we have chosen to translate *maquinismo* as "mechanism" in order to emphasize the connection between machinism and the mechanization of life that underwrites it, and because what Ramos is referring to by "machinism" can now also be applied to the computerization of the world.]

distinguishes the human animal from the rest of the animal kingdom is that the mental instruments we use to satisfy our biological needs are more sophisticated. As part of this view, "determinism" subjects the will to mechanical causes and, consequently, rejects moral autonomy. If there is such a thing as "class ideology," this materialist conception of humanity is the most genuine expression of bourgeois psychology. The origin of this ideology dates back to the English philosopher Thomas Hobbes, but it wasn't fully developed until the nineteenth century, first in the philosophy of [Ludwig] Feuerbach and later in every thinker who applied the scientific method to understanding mental life. In the last century, this conception of the human being was made widely popular in connection with Darwin's theory of evolution and as one of the basic theses of "materialist monism," as presented by [Ludwig] Büchner and [Ernst] Haeckel.[6]

It is no surprise that everyone was quick to turn this idea into established truth, since, even if it lacks scientific rigor, it appeals to our most powerful instincts. Herein lies the secret of its "proof" and dogmatic tone. Since this idea serves our most energetic vital impulses, we inevitably endorse it as passionately as possible. However, what is certain is that if we consider the consequences of that idea objectively, we will realize that it has led to the debasement of human values. Let us not confuse the naturalist conception of the human being with another set of ideas that, under a similar guise, have the opposite goal of ennobling instinct and freeing it from the unjust condemnation leveled against it by the spiritualist's asceticism. This is the great ambition of vitalist philosophy, represented by thinkers such as [Wilhelm] Dilthey, Nietzsche, and Bergson, when they attribute a psychic category to life, a move in which there pulsates a new valuation of the human being.

Despite everything, we are not satisfied with the naturalist's way of valuing of our own existence. In practice, the happiness for which we hope seems to have escaped us, and in the midst of all the stimulation

---

6. [See Ludwig Büchner, *Force and Matter: Empirico-Philosophical Studies Intelligibly Rendered* (London: Trübner & Co., 1870); and Ernst Haeckel, *Monism as Connecting Religion and Science: The Confession of Faith of a Man of Science* (London: Adam and Charles Black, 1895).]

material life has to offer, we occasionally have the terrible feeling that we are empty inside. It is the feeling of *nothingness* that Kierkegaard describes in his critique of modern civilization. On our psychoanalytic account, the preoccupations with material life are unable to destroy the spiritual depth of humans; they have only been able to tune it out. Now it is matter that represses the spirit. Matter has not reestablished the harmony and balance of human nature; it has only inverted the ancient state of things without correcting its extremism.

Our inner imbalance has undermined the confidence and admiration that we once felt toward our spectacular civilization, and we developed a pessimism which led to a philosophy that negates the values of civilization. The precursor of this stance against civilization can be found in Rousseau who, in response to a question posed by the Academy of Dijon (1750), said that "our minds have been corrupted in proportion as the arts and sciences have improved."[7] Pessimists consider civilization a symptom of the decline of the human being and have offered compelling evidence in support of this position. However, this conception of the human, which [Max] Scheler has called a "misguided idea," is far from being widely held.[8] Nietzsche also endorses this opinion when he claims that the person who lives a "decadent life" erects civilization as a device to compensate for their

---

7. [Jean-Jacques Rousseau, *The Social Contract & Discourses*, trans. G. D. H. Cole (London and Toronto: J. M. Dent & Sons, 1913), 133.]

8. [Ramos is likely referring to Max Scheler, *The Human Place in the Cosmos*, trans. Manfred Frings (Evanston, IL: Northwestern University Press, 2009 [1928]). Max Scheler's theory of values had been enthusiastically endorsed by José Ortega y Gasset, who commissioned several translations for his *Revista de Occidente*. Upon Scheler's death in 1928, Ortega wrote: "La muerte de Max Scheler deja a Europa sin la mente mejor que poseía, donde nuestro tiempo gozaba en reflejarse con pasmosa precisión. Ahora es preciso completar su esfuerzo añadiendo lo que le faltó, arquitectura, orden sistema." ("The death of Max Scheler has left Europe without its best mind, a mind that reflected our time with incredible decision. Now it is necessary to complete his effort, lending it what it lacked: structure, order, system.") José Ortega y Gasset, "Max Scheler, un embriagado de esencias," in *Obras Completas*, vol. 4 (Madrid: Revista de Occidente, 1966), 511.]

decline.⁹ What is the human being according to this conception? *A defector of life* who employs surrogates to stand in for authentic vital functions. Science, technology, tools, and machines are a lengthy detour that we pursue to obtain what we need, since biological weakness prevents us from getting what we need directly, as other animals do. The human is a sick animal because we do not know, directly or unequivocally, what to do or where to go. For some thinkers, such as [Ludwig] Klages, who strongly endorses vital values,¹⁰ the spirit is a diabolical power that destroys and annihilates life and the soul. Life and spirit, then, are presented as two totally antagonistic forces. Pessimism was brought to a crisis in the widespread ideas of [Oswald] Spengler, which are summarized in his famous theory of the "decline of the West."

Without admitting, of course, that the human being truly is in decline, much less that our decline arises from our essence, there is no doubt that our contemporary crisis reveals that there is something wrong in the organization of life and in our innermost attitude toward it. We will not dwell here on the critique of economic organization, not because we are unfamiliar with the importance of this factor of life, but because, thanks to socialist propaganda, those ideas are already well known and we would not be able to say anything new about it. For now, we will limit ourselves to showing that there are also certain psychological factors that contribute decisively to the crisis of the modern human being, which requires spiritual reform as an indispensable condition in the effort to restore the equilibrium of our being.¹¹ Reform is possible when humans examine their

---

9. [See, for example, Friedrich Nietzsche, *On the Genealogy of Morality*, ed. Keith Ansell Pearson, trans. Carol Diethe (Cambridge: Cambridge University Press, 2007).]

10. [See Ludwig Klages, *Der Geist als Widersacher der Seele* [The Spirit as Adversary of the Soul] (Leipzig: Johan Ambrosius Barth, 1929).]

11. [The notion of a "spiritual reform" echoes, to a certain extent, José Ortega y Gasset's call to "reform the intellect" or reform our way of thinking. In Ortega's view, the power of the mind should not be reduced to utilitarian ends, such as political change, but should preserve its autonomy in theory. "De aquí la grave crisis del presente, que se caracteriza no tanto porque no se obedezca a principios

consciousness and discover that the root of this evil is an internal contradiction. Every contradiction contains within it the drive to be resolved, which is another way of saying that what modern humans lack is not the will to reform themselves, but the knowledge of the most reliable means to carry out this reform.

The discontent of modern consciousness indicates a lack of harmony between the human being and the world. Civilization has profoundly complicated life to the point that we are disoriented among the multiplicity of things that we invented ourselves. A disorientation that consists fundamentally in a false mental outlook that distorts the sense of values and upsets the natural order of things in terms of their importance.

One error of valuation that has had the most unfavorable consequences is that of *elevating the means to the status of ends*. In the service of the value of "power," the intellect has invented remarkable scientific techniques without precedent in history. In view of our marvelous achievements, we wound up overestimating the importance of technical problems and forgetting the true end they serve. All the activities of life and culture have suffered because of this mistake. In art, science, industry, and economy, examples of this disastrous estimation abound. Nowadays, given the naive admiration of art lovers, artworks of extremely dubious quality but which are produced with dazzling and ingenious technique are often passed off as masterpieces. Science and philosophy have not escaped the harmful influence of this modern fetishism. As [Georg] Simmel says:

> In this way, what could be called superfluous knowledge is accumulating in many areas of scholarship and science—a sum of methodologically faultless knowledge, unassailable from the standpoint of an abstract concept of knowledge, but nonetheless alienated from the genuine purpose and meaning of all research. Here it goes without

---

superiores sino por la ausencia de éstos." (This gives rise to the present crisis, which is characterized not so much because superior principles aren't obeyed but because there aren't any.) José Ortega y Gasset, "La reforma de la inteligencia," in *Obras completas*, vol. 4 (Madrid: Revista de Occidente, 1966 [1926]), 498.]

saying, I am referring to the ideal and universal purpose of all research, not an external purpose.

[. . .] This is the basis of the fetishistic worship which for a long time has been conducted with regard to "method"—as if an achievement were valuable simply because of the correctness of its method. This is a very clever means for the legitimation and appreciation of an unlimited number of works which are invalid for the meaning and context of the advancement of knowledge, no matter how generously the latter is framed.[12]

The consequence of the worship of technology is *overproduction*,[13] which unnecessarily multiplies the variety and volume of culture and civilization to the point that we are oppressed by its overwhelming weight. This multitude of things artificially increases our needs and presents us with new obligations every day. The fever for technology

> explains the industrial manufacture of certain products for which no need actually exists; yet the constraint of fully utilizing already existing installations pushes for this; the technical scale demands of its own accord to be completed by links, which the psychological scale—actually the definite one—does not require, and that is how the supply of commodities comes into existence, commodities which for their own part are only artificial and which, when viewed from the standpoint of the culture of human subjects, call forth meaningless needs.[14]

Up to a point, production is under the control of the will, but later it develops its own impetus for growth, which drags us down; the result is that we become the dominated instead of the dominator. Having completely surrendered to the external world, concerned only with

---

12. Simmel, *La tragedia de la cultura*. [Georg Simmel, "The Concept and Tragedy of Culture," in *Simmel on Culture: Selected Writings*, ed. David Frisby and Mike Featherstone, trans. Mark Ritter and David Frisby (London: Sage, 1997), 71.]
13. [*Overproduction* is italicized in the original.]
14. Simmel, "The Concept and Tragedy of Culture," 70–71.

material issues that displace all other interests, the life of the soul is slowly extinguished until the individual becomes an automaton.

Certain sensible spirits rebel against the thinning of the air that threatens to suffocate the life of the soul. In a conversation between two Russian intellectuals shut away in a health clinic, some written reflections represent a beautiful document that captures the discomfort of the contemporary consciousness. One writes: "Your acute sense that the cultural heritage you bear is an enormous burden derives essentially from experiencing culture not as a living treasury of gifts, but as a system of the subtlest compulsions. No wonder: for culture has actually attempted to become a system of convulsions" (Gerchenson).[15] The other writer launches his protest with these words:

> Finally, there are the countless results of knowledge, terrible in their multiplicity and inexorableness; they inundate the mind, establishing themselves within it as objective truth without waiting till hunger summons those among them which are really needed; and the spirit, crushed by their weight, withers in its overcrowded quarters, powerless either to appropriate them in an authentic manner or to expel them. Consequently, I speak not of freedom from theory, but of freedom of theory, or more accurately, of freedom, directness, and freshness of contemplation (Ivanov).[16]

In this passage one of the conflicts that afflicts contemporary consciousness is expressed with great clarity. Civilization has deprived the individual of their liberty; with multiple restraints, it has trapped their spirit; and it has imposed upon them a strange personality. The individual's own will, one's feelings, aspirations, vocation, strength are rendered impotent under the mask that the external world has placed on us.

---

15. Gerchenson and Ivanov, *Desde un ángulo a otro*. [Letter III, from Ivanov to Gershenson, in "A Correspondence Between Two Corners," trans. Norbert Guterman, *Partisan Review* 9 (September, 1948): 955.]

16. [Letter VIII, from Gershenson to Ivanov, 1033.]

Among the detailed observations that abound in the philosophy of Bergson, which are sometimes more valuable than his fundamental doctrine, one observation captures the true psychology of the modern human. According to Bergson, the human soul is made up of two layers that correspond to two different "selves." There is a peripheral layer into which the individual deposits the experience acquired through practical action; in a way, it is the result of the individual adapting to their environment. This is the *social self*. Beneath this layer, at the center of the soul, there is the *profound self* which virtually contains individual potentialities that do not have a useful application, but which instead are the better part of the subject, that which is most properly one's own, the nucleus of one's noblest activities, those that might flower into a spiritual personality.

> Hence there are finally two different selves, one of which is, as it were, the external projection of the other, its spatial and, so to speak, social representation. We reach the former by deep introspection, which leads us to grasp our inner states as living things, constantly *becoming* [. . .]. But the moments at which we thus grasp ourselves are rare, and that is just why we are rarely free. The greater part of the time we live outside ourselves, hardly perceiving anything of ourselves, but our own ghost, a colourless shadow [. . .]; we live for the external world rather than for ourselves; we speak rather than think; we "are acted" rather than act ourselves. To act freely is to recover possession of oneself.[17]

The two selves in the Bergsonian doctrine correspond to two different moments of life. The social self is the past, what has already been lived. The profound self is the present and the future, the creative force in potential, what has not yet been lived. That is why the social self is something dead while the profound self represents what is still living in the human being.

Many individuals still ignore this subterranean region of the soul, and the mission of art is to reveal it. We can explain aesthetic pleasure

---

17. Henri Bergson, *Essai sur les données immédiates de la conscience*, p. 178. [*Time and Free Will: An Essay on the Immediate Data of Consciousness*, trans. F. L. Pogson (London: George Allen & Unwin, 1950), 231–32.]

precisely because when the artist lifts off the crust of our spirit to contemplate its depths, we recognize our most intimate self; we contemplate what we might otherwise have been but are not on account of other, more pressing demands. The drama that accompanies dualism is an inexhaustible theme for theater, and it has inspired, in effect, some of [Luigi] Pirandello's greatest plays.[18] The destiny that annihilated Greek heroes is represented here by an implacable social force that imposes on individuals a contradictory personality; those heroes were exhausted by a futile fight to shake it off. They are not human beings but characters that in the end succumb to the false role that life obliges them to represent.

Our tragedy today is that our material and ideal creations rebel against us. The vast world of civilization and culture acquires an independent dynamism that moves along a path different from that which we should travel. Pulled out of our own trajectory, our liberty annulled, the human gradually loses their characteristic attributes, precisely those in which human dignity is found, and we downgrade the rank of our existence. Not all of us are fully aware of what is happening, but the majority do feel a discontent that keeps them in constant rebellion without a definite aim, striving for something they are unable to find because they do not know what it is. However, many of us have discovered the cause of the disquietude and are aware that the status of the human is at low tide. Civilization, such as it is organized, seems like a diabolic plan to leave humans without souls and convert them into a specter of what they used to be in better times. Everything we produce in the material or ideal realm, for our own benefit, turns out to be counterproductive, and sooner or later, our creations are like potions that subjugate and paralyze the movements of the soul. Here is an eloquent description of this phenomenon:

> Everyone knew that Napoleon was not born an Emperor. A simple woman seeing him from the crowd during some splendid parade, might have thought: "Now he is the Emperor who almost lost his personal name, he is the ruler of nations—yet in his swaddling clothes

---

18. [See Samuel Ramos, "Teatro: Pirandello," in *Obras Completas*, vol. 1 (México City: Universidad Nacional Autónoma de México, 1975), 260–62.]

he was nothing to the world, only another child of his mother's."—Similarly, when I stand in a museum before a famous painting, I think to myself the artist painted it for himself, and in the act of creation it was inseparable from him—he was in it and in him; yet now it has been elevated to the world throne, as an objective value....

Everything that is objective is conceived in the individual and originally belongs only to him. Whatever value is in question, its biography comprises the same three phases that Napoleon went through: First, it is nothing for the world, then it is a warrior and leader on the battlefield, finally a ruler. Finally, this utility becomes a generally accepted value, and the value receives the royal crown. The crowned value is cold and cruel, and in the course of years it completely petrifies, turns into a fetish.... Now it autocratically dictates its laws to the world, heedless of individual prayers.... What was alive and individual, immersed in, and fed on, one man's blood, now becomes an idol, which demands that living people, similar to what it itself was when it came into the world, be sacrificed to it. Napoleon as emperor and a painting enthroned in a museum are equally despotic.[19]

The same author uses a happy parable to flesh out the history of values that, as they accumulate, become harmful to human development:

> The deer developed antlers by virtue of an inherent law, as a means of self-defense and intimidation of his enemies; but in some species of deer the antlers reached such a size that they impeded the animal in his flight through the woods, and the species died out.

---

19. *Desde un ángulo a otro*. [Letter VIII, from Gershenson to Ivanov, in "A Correspondence Between Two Corners," *op. cit.*, 1030–31. The ellipses are in the original. Also, in *Hacia un nuevo humanismo*, Ramos includes a passage that the translator could not find in the *Partisan Review*: "No se puede describir más bellamente ese proceso de deshumanización de la cultura que hoy padece la humanidad y le arrebata sus mejores atributos. Cuando un individuo a costa de sacrificios ha logrado crear un valor nuevo, su premio es que le arranquen su criatura para hacerle patrimonio universal." Our best guess is that Ramos put quotes around his own words, falsely suggesting they are part of the conversation between Ivanov and Gershenson. It makes more sense to read this sentence as Ramos commenting on the passages, saying that "One cannot describe more beautifully that process of the dehumanization of culture that the human being suffers today."]

Is not the situation of culture the same? Are not our "values" something like these antlers—at first the result of individual adaptation, then the general possession of the race, and finally a burden and impediment that has grown enormously, and become tormenting, even fatal for the individual?[20]

After a grueling secular effort, the human being was surrounded by countless things, ideas, and values that obstructed their way, and they felt lost in an artificial forest that they planted and cultivated with their own hands. We might have hoped to raise ourselves above nature in search of space that was freer, but what is certain is that one's back is now hunched under the weight of a complicated world that we have not figured out how to dominate. Material labor and economic struggle were carried out inside a vicious organization that is perhaps one of the most powerful factors in the degradation of the human being. One might encounter the feeling of human dignity, which protests in anguish from its vital depths, deep in the socialist criticisms of capitalism.[21] A quote from the economist Sombart is enough to explain how capitalism is detrimental to human values:

> We have already seen that the bourgeois spirit of our age is utterly careless of man's fate. We noted how man is no longer the central fact of economic activities and economic thought. It is only the procedure that matters—production, transport, price formation. In a word, *Fiat productio et pereat homo*.[22]

---

20. [Letter VIII, from Gershenson to Ivanov, 1040.]
21. This interpretation is confirmed by Marxism. "Marx was not a utilitarian. [...] He condemns capitalism not because it makes people unhappy but because it makes them *inhuman*, deprives them of their essential dignity, degrades all their ideals by setting a cash value on them, and inflicts *meaningless* suffering." Sidney Hook, *Pour comprendre Marx*, Gallimard, 1936, p. 86. [Sidney Hook, *Towards the Understanding of Karl Marx: A Revolutionary Interpretation* (London: Victor Gollancz, 1933), chap. 9]
22. W. Sombart: *Le Bourgeois*. [*The Quintessence of Capitalism*, 330–31.]

Given everything so far, we can conclude that the fundamental values of humanism are in crisis. The problems surrounding humanism are not only aesthetic or academic, but also profoundly moral, and morality cannot be left out of the full reorganization of society if we are serious about improving the current conditions of existence. It is clear that the future organization of society ought to be worked out in view of the well-being and happiness of everyone, regardless of class, correcting all the injustices of today. But we cannot fully achieve this goal if we do not take into account the totality of human aspirations. Today humanism emerges as an ideal to combat the subhumanity brought about by bourgeois capitalism and materialism. The consciousness of countless beings, barely aware of the degradation of their nature, are induced by the rank air they breathe, and therefore the most enlightened spirits are obliged to denounce the demoralization that the human suffers. It is up to the youth who seek a better and more just society, more generally it is up to everyone who has the will to create a new world, to affirm and defend the values of humanism. But a serious question remains to be answered: What *ought* the human *to be*?

There is no easy answer. It is a question that has always troubled humankind, which has tried to solve it along different routes. While there are more immediate and pressing problems, this question is still of vital importance. We would have to be careless and confused not to take an interest in reflecting on the destiny of humanity. It is precisely during times of crisis and catastrophe like ours that the consciousness of humanity withdraws in the attempt to probe the enigma of life. Knowledge of the human being is today at the center of philosophical reflection, making use of every intellectual resource. To ensure its results, it is necessary, beforehand, to spell out a rigorous method of analyzing and measuring the possibilities of knowledge as they apply to the sphere of anthropological problems. The aim of this small book is not to examine these problems in their entirety, but to set an agenda in agreement with the current state of philosophical anthropology, which raises questions and suggests how today's thought tries to answer them.

CHAPTER TWO

On the Concept of Philosophy

We are currently living through a time of crisis that touches every aspect of human existence and which, in the realm of spirit, has sown confusion in ideas and values. It is important to acknowledge that contemporary philosophy has examined this global crisis tirelessly and has successfully revealed different paths toward salvation.[1] The presupposition of such theories is that salvation depends not only on a change in material conditions, but also, at the same time, on rebuilding our spiritual world. The themes discussed in this work relate to problems that everyone ought to take seriously nowadays. The task of philosophy is now more burdensome than ever, since the times we live in are extremely problematic. Human destiny, the social and individual forms of human existence, and the substance of civilization and culture, are the subject of passionate debate, one that allows for widely divergent points of view. Philosophy exists because there are certain problems of a general nature that do not belong to the domain of religion or the particular sciences, but to a discipline that, with a higher plan, tries to encompass all of reality under a comprehensive vision. The first phase of philosophy is to make itself aware of these problems by raising and accurately describing them. For a shallow mind who believes that it already possesses the truth, that is, one that is completely unaware that there is a problem, philosophy is unnecessary.

---

1. [Despite its religious connotations, the term *salvation* is reminiscent of Ortega's philosophy and his famous dictum: "I am myself and my circumstances; and if I don't save it, I do not save myself." In this context, *salvation* has at least two meanings: preservation from danger and knowing something by situating it as part of a whole. See José Ortega y Gasset, *Meditations on Quixote*, trans. Evelyn Rugg and Diego Marín (Urbana and Chicago: University of Illinois Press, 1961 [1914]).]

17

The ideas presented in this book are a summary of the author's philosophical convictions. The exposition was born from a kind of self-examination, a liquidation of ideas, undertaken in order to participate in a philosophical debate taking place in the contemporary world. Although a critical spirit would advise reserving a modicum of doubt concerning any theory, never accepting it absolutely, we in fact always prefer one theory over another because it seems to answer the problems of philosophy more satisfactorily. This book should be considered a sincere attempt to comprehend the philosophical currents that are most relevant to contemporary thought. Philosophy subsists not only on the creation of original ideas, but also on the more modest act of rethinking what has already been thought, on the mental reproduction of the entire process of philosophical speculation that, in a way, is a recreation of philosophy. This is the only method that leads to the world of philosophy and to unlocking its secrets.

The aim of these chapters is not to produce a philosophical treatise that presents its problems systematically. They should be read only as a selection of philosophical ideas arranged according to a personal perspective. I believe that all philosophical questions flow from one central problem that is more or less the focus of speculative interest: the human being and our world. It seems to me that a certain conception of being human is presupposed by the various theories of knowledge, morality, art, history, etc. Systematic exposition should trace the actual trajectory of philosophical thought with an open mind, beginning with an ontology of human life and moving on to problems that are further removed from the human being but that eventually lead back to their point of departure. Only by going full circle does thought get fleshed out and is it able, in the end, to confirm with certainty what at the beginning was merely a hypothesis.

That is, when we begin to philosophize, we do not know much about ourselves, only what the immediate intuition of our lives teaches us. But upon going full circle, we know infinitely more; we acquire full consciousness of ourselves. By thinking of philosophy in this way, it appears to be more than a cognitive instrument, more than simply a theoretical attitude. The human is never a finished being, but a process on the path to realization whose impulse is born from within. In other words, the human is a being that constantly strives toward goals that we are capable of representing to ourselves in the form of an idea.

Now, insofar as philosophy is able to define these goals in advance, it appears to serve a vital function that contributes to the fulfillment of the human being. In this sense, philosophy is an investigation of normative consciousness, and its mission is not limited to understanding the human being empirically, but extends to understanding the *idea* of being human, understanding what a human being ought to be. This last proposition can be understood in two equally valid ways. Within a global perspective, it can be understood as the definition of the essence of *being human*, bracketing out empirical manifestations. Or, within a particular perspective, it can be understood as a determination of the different forms of human consciousness, scientific consciousness, ethical, aesthetic, etc. That is how [Wilhelm] Windelband defines philosophy, as the knowledge of normative consciousness and of the values that ground its legitimacy.[2]

If it is true that these various activities refer to objects that exist in the world, and true that philosophy should consider them as well, then at the other end it is true that the human being is the universal subject of these activities, the subject of knowledge, the subject of history, of culture, etc. For this reason, the various questions that philosophy treats as independent must culminate in the knowledge of the human being, that is, in philosophical anthropology.

Origin of the Notion of Reality

As soon as human consciousness is awakened, it finds itself surrounded by a myriad of people, things, events—completely disordered at first, like objects that parade around utterly disconnected. But as knowledge and experience gradually develop over the course of life, the individual notices relations among objects and slowly begins to sort them into groups that, in turn, are integrated into the idea of a whole world. When we achieve this fullness of consciousness, we assume our position in the world and feel as though we exist as

---

2. [Wilhelm Windelband, *Logic*, trans. B. E. Meyer (London: Macmillan, 1913).]

part of a totality. So, our being presents itself as a notion of the world that contains us. The notion of being has two dimensions: one spatial and one temporal. This notion is not complete until it is situated at a certain point in space and time. Existence appears at the intersection of two coordinates, an ideal one that comes from the historical world and a material one from the physical world. But before the world is given as a totality, there exists for each of us only a smaller world, the world of persons and things close to us, those that surround our actual existence. Unavoidably, we are familiar only with the totality of the world through, or from the point of view of, the small world that surrounds us. The repertoire of our lived experiences is limited to this smaller world; only here are we able to establish direct connections.

We can assume different attitudes toward the elements that make up the surrounding world. The same thing can be the object of our will, of our feeling, or of our knowledge. To decide which of these relations is basic, the observation that we can't but live before engaging in theoretical knowledge will suffice. Our first interactions with the world are practical in nature; things first appear as the object of our needs. However, those interactions are essential to subsequent relations, such as the knowledge-relation. Sooner or later, opposition, conflict, and struggle appear in practical life. The world reveals itself as something unruly, something that resists our interests and desires. It exists as something foreign that carries on independently of our will. Thus, one begins to feel, one begins to acquire sufficient proof, that the world exists as a reality in itself, exists in a manner different from ours. Through this vital experience, then, the notion of reality emerges.

Metaphysical Assumptions of Idealism

The notion of a reality that exists in itself, as something foreign, gives rise to the need for knowledge. Idealism has tried to eliminate the notion of reality in itself as an indemonstrable and useless hypothesis.[3] But in doing so, it overlooks the very essence of the

---

3. [In *Lecciones Preliminares de Filosofía*, a popular introduction to philosophy in the late 1930s still in print today, Manuel García Morente presents the history of Western philosophy in terms of the antithesis between realism and idealism.

knowledge-relation. It believes it can give an account of knowledge as the simple coherence of thoughts in a "unity of meaning," indifferent to whether objects exist or not. Can we call the consciousness of something that does not exist in itself knowledge? If knowledge is not the conception of realities that actually exist, if reality is composed in and for the act of knowing, what is the difference between knowledge and fantasy? It is true that objects are given only in knowledge, but it does not follow that they exist only in knowledge. Claiming that objects exist only as the content of consciousness is just a play on words, since the contents of consciousness are not objects but representations.

The existence of a reality that subsists in itself is the assumption required to make sense of the knowledge-relation. Every relation presupposes that there are two terms, which in the case of knowledge are represented by a subject and an object. Idealism—though it does not want to admit it—suppresses one of the terms and turns the object into a product of pure subjectivity. It is true that idealism attributes the object to a "transcendental consciousness," but if there is such consciousness, it exists only in the subject. Therefore, idealism is ultimately a form of subjectivism.

Moreover, if reality doesn't exist in itself, the values of truth and falsity don't make sense. If thought doesn't correspond to real objects, there is no basis whatsoever upon which to predicate truth or falsity.

That is, while García Morente uses both "realism" and "idealism" to refer to particular theses and schools, as in the phrase "post-Kantian idealism," he also uses the terms to refer more broadly to the split between ancient and modern philosophy, where the view that fundamental reality is something other than the world of appearances (i.e., "realism") characterizes philosophy from Parmenides to Aristotle, and the view that there is no fundamental reality, at least not that we can know of, other than human subjectivity (i.e., "idealism") characterizes philosophy from Descartes through the post-Kantian idealists (roughly until 1900). The aim of contemporary philosophy, or the new "existential" account of reality, as represented by philosophers such as Dilthey, Heidegger, Ortega y Gasset, is to reconcile the antithesis between realism and idealism—broadly understood—in the form of a view of reality that encompasses both subject and object, theory and life. Contemporary philosophy, in this sense, ought to be considered a "philosophy of life." (See "The 'Toward' of Samuel Ramos.")]

Nobody claims that truth consists purely in the agreement between thought and a certain logical validity—with the *logos*—because, if that were so, what grounds the authority of the *logos*? Or should that authority be granted blindly? Eliminating the concept of reality forces idealists to distort the original meaning of the phenomenon of knowledge, designating by this name something that it doesn't really deserve. If idealists believe that by eliminating the notion of reality, they cleanse the problem of knowledge of all metaphysical baggage, they unwittingly raise other questions no less metaphysical. Idealism is not free from metaphysical assumptions, as it aspires to be. Knowledge is always knowledge of something and that something is a real object. This conviction also applies to cognitive activity. If idealism thinks that cognitive activity is an illusion, it must explain how that illusion is produced. Is the illusion a coincidental, unmotivated phenomenon? If the conviction of realism is illusory, then what we take for reality is mere appearance. But why do our ideas appear to be of reality? Why don't we take appearance as appearance? Why don't we assume the same attitude toward science as we do toward art? The very idea of appearance implies the existence of a reality that is able to appear. Appearance and reality are correlative ideas, the one cannot exist without the other. Appearance is the appearance of something that is not just an appearance. If all knowledge only has an ideal existence, what is ideal existence? Isn't ideal existence an enigma as indecipherable as real existence? In the end, the foundation of both ideal existence and real existence must draw from the same source: intuition.

The Ontological Foundation of Knowledge

To understand in what sense the knowledge-relation is transcendent, that is, how it leads beyond consciousness, one must take into account that this relation is not the only bridge between humans and reality. Before knowledge, humans are bound, existentially integrated into the world. What I call "my existence" does not include only the existence of my individual body or mind, but also a ring of real things that coexist with them. The world that surrounds me is part of me, not something foreign to my existence. This salient aspect of human ontology clears away many uncertainties in the theory of knowledge, especially the problem of transcendence. As a theory, idealism will always flagrantly contradict the immediate experience of life. Its adherents will never be able to reconcile their theoretical convictions with the facts of practical life. The incongruities of idealism stem from a false ontological assumption implicit in its assertions: the human being is primarily a theoretical entity destined to pursue pure knowledge. The conclusions of idealism would be valid if an intellectualist conception of being were true, namely one that reduces the human being to an abstraction, a logical phantasm. A conception so conceived, completely unsupported, will never ground or explain existence. Existence is not subordinate to thought; on the contrary, as Descartes discovered in his *Meditations on First Philosophy*, it goes the other way around. The correct interpretation of the Cartesian principle confirms everything we have said so far. At bottom, what Descartes wanted to say was: How can I doubt and think if I do not first exist? And the confirmation will be even stronger if by "thought" we take into account all the connotations of the French word *pensée*. "Mais qu'est-ce donc que je suis? Une chose qui pense. Qu'est-ce qu'une chose qui pense? C'est une chose qui doute, qui entend, qui conçoit, qui affirme, qui nie, qui veut, qui ne veut pas, qu'imagine aussi et qui sent."[4]

Based on the conception of the human being as existentially integrated into their surrounding world, we can conclude with confidence that what one knows best in close detail belongs to the surrounding ring of real things. I am not saying that human beings can know only what is closest to them, but that broader and more general knowledge must be filtered through the perspective of what is near. As part of their existence, each individual possesses a concrete world, which is the sole window at one's disposal to peer out into the general world.

---

4. ["But what therefore am I? A thinking thing. What is that? I mean a thing that doubts, that understands, that affirms, that denies, that wishes to do this and does not wish to do that, and also that imagines and perceives by the senses." René Descartes, *Meditations on First Philosophy: With Selections from the Objections and Replies*, trans. Michael Moriarty (Oxford: Oxford University Press, 2008), 20.]

That is to say, what each subject knows better than anyone else is the natural landscape they inhabit, one's society, one's own country. One knows these things from within, so to speak, because they make up half of oneself; one is vitally fused with them. These concrete objects must of necessity be the particular instances that give life and color to the generic concepts of the universe, humanity, or society. Despite their objective value, whenever we think about ideas independent of space and time, we must refer to them, like it or not, through the circle of our immediate experience. This is doubtless a limitation on our knowledge, but, at the same time, it is also an advantage, that of discovering in the world something that no one else is ever in a position to see.

The Variation of the Categories

I do not deny that there is a logical structure common to humankind, or at least to civilized human beings, or that there are objective norms of knowledge. The relativism that we have highlighted refers to the particular applications of the intellect and to a preference for certain ideas. I know that many of us share the same environment and that in the end all human beings inhabit one world. But it is also undeniable that there are peculiar modalities to certain places on the planet and moments in history, specific problems of every kind that emerge from the varying circumstances of human life. Now, the whole set of particular circumstances that presses upon each individual makes one more interested in certain bits of knowledge to which others are indifferent. Therefore, the vital circumstance makes a selection of interests in accordance with which the intellect directs its goals. That selection alone is enough to give our scientific and philosophical repertoire its particular physiognomy, recognizing that individual points of view can be that of a person, a people, or an epoch. As a matter of fact, this is how science and philosophy have always been practiced and the relativity of a point of view is a necessary condition nobody can escape, however hard they try. What is inconceivable is the possibility of a thought that is conceived from no point of view.

The critique of knowledge has established that we can think about reality only through a certain mental structure composed of *a priori* forms, categories of knowledge, which are like a grid that is projected onto the world in order to make it intelligible. These categories are *first principles* with explanatory power; however, they cannot themselves be explained because they would cease to be first principles. The Kantian theory of knowledge starts with a subject's consciousness as though it were an absolute beginning. The notion of an existential unity between the human being and the world leads us to interpret things differently [from Kant]. Nothing about Kantianism stops us from thinking that if the system of categories were different, knowledge might be structured under a different, equally valid scientific form. But this assumption is impossible in our view. If there is a perfect correspondence between the categories and reality, it is because our intellect gives back what it takes from reality. The intellect is geometric; it has been formed through an interaction with solids, as Bergson says, and this prolonged exchange leaves an indelible mark, the shape of space, within which we must frame our notions if they are to be intelligible.[5] I mention this briefly so as to suggest how the comprehensive system of categories ought to be explained. Without fully agreeing with Bergson's theory of knowledge, it seems to me that the principle on which it is grounded is correct. Bergson says, "A theory of knowledge which does not replace the intellect in the general evolution of life will teach us neither how the frames of knowledge have been constructed nor how we can enlarge or go beyond them. It is necessary that these two inquiries, theory of knowledge and theory of life, should join each other, and, by a circular process, push each other on unceasingly."[6]

Kant's system of categories is valid only for mathematics and physics. It gives priority to the logical constitution of the human being because the knowledge of physical nature has been successfully

---

5. [Henri Bergson, *Creative Evolution*, trans. Arthur Mitchel (New York: Henry Holt and Company, 1911), chap. 3, https://www.gutenberg.org/files/26163/26163-h/26163-h.htm.]

6. [Bergson, *Creative Evolution*, xiv.]

cultivated and developed for centuries. The lack of a critical consciousness of the categories, which might have determined the boundaries of their valid application, has led to the mistake of extending them to other areas of knowledge and distorting their respective ideas. The error was made worse by the assumption that reality is everywhere one and the same, and the assumption that all of reality is governed by the same laws, and consequently that everything can be explained by the same intellectual principles. Thus, an abstract and geometric unity of the universe was postulated. Such was the case when the principles of natural science were applied to the human sciences [*las ciencias del espíritu*[7]] and to the science of history. Now that we have discovered this error, we know that each particular area of experience should be explained by a unique set of categories taken from a particular area of knowledge.[8] A superior knowledge of the universe shows that it is more accurate to presuppose a plurality of orders, each one ruled by a peculiar set of laws. We know that the repertoire of categories is not fixed or immutable but changes with the epochs of history. Categories are not, as Kant supposed, the pure emanation of the subject who, upon producing knowledge, acts as the "legislator of the Universe." The assumption must be that the intellect is a malleable instrument subject to constant reform, shaped by the very experience that dictates the right form of intellection. The subject does nothing but select and employ these given principles in accordance with

---

7. ["Ciencias del espíritu" refers to the classic German distinction between Geistes and Naturwissenschaften, a classification of knowledge made famous by Friedrich Schleiermacher and Wilhelm Dilthey, and widely used at the time when Ramos was writing.]

8. [Another close reader of Dilthey, Ortega y Gasset also noted the progressive autonomy of, and specialization in, all fields of knowledge: "In the new attitude of those sciences which prefer to withdraw each into its own corner, its own orbit, is there not the mark of a new human sensitiveness which tries to resolve the problem of life by a method the reverse of that which prevailed earlier? A method in which each being and each occupation accepts its own destiny, drives deep into it, and rather than indulging in the illusion of moving elsewhere, fills its own authentic and untransferable outline to the very edges?" José Ortega y Gasset, *What Is Philosophy?*, trans. Mildred Adams (New York: Norton Library, 1960), 55.]

the scientific exigencies of the day. The frameworks of knowledge are the result of an agreement between certain interests and particular demands of the intellect, on the one hand, and reality with its own manner of being, on the other.

Intuition and Categories

Without a doubt, the greatest obstacle to turning reason into a malleable instrument that adapts to the various problems of reality has been the very progress of science. The more bits of knowledge humans accumulate, the more prejudices threaten to hinder their way as they continue to explore new sectors of reality. The crisis of science and philosophy can be attributed, in part, to the excessive accumulation of knowledge that eventually becomes a burden and hindrance to the development of the intellect itself. For one thing, countless framework assumptions act as prejudices; for another, they turn into a form of inertia: acquired mental habits tend to turn the intellect into a rigid instrument that lends an artificial character to its procedures. The importance placed on questions of method leads one to overestimate the technical side of knowledge, bestowing upon it the value of an end, and that is how reason, excessively proud of itself, becomes the reality that it is supposed to explain. A reason that understands its true mission should be a transparent medium, invisible, so that its gaze is allowed to sweep over the objects beyond the subject. This is not the attitude that various forms of intellectualism, especially idealism, take toward reason.

The only solution to the problem is to suspend, for a moment, the weight of acquired knowledge, in order to experience reality directly, to make unmediated contact with it by means of intuition. In my opinion, this is the meaning and value of Husserl's phenomenological method, which recommends intuiting essences pre-theoretically before all judgment or reason. This is the value of the "phenomenological reduction," that is, the approach that "puts in parentheses" the reality of objects under consideration, as well as everything we know or can know about them.⁹ If one of the aspirations of phenomenology is to obtain knowledge free of prejudice, it is of first-rate importance and value in the effort to combat the contemporary crisis of science. Under these conditions, intuition is an indispensable resource that puts us back in direct contact with real things—not as the only cognitive instrument, to be sure, but certainly as an aid to reason. It gives reason the explanatory principles and the categories it needs in new areas of science, those that it would try to understand using ideas borrowed from other sciences. Understood as direct evidence of certain basic truths, intuition must serve as the sole criterion for discovering and choosing the indispensable *a priori* [principles] to orient the intellect on future travels. Intuition should be the basis upon which to vitalize reason, revising reason as often as is required by changes in the circumstances in which it is inevitably employed.

The reform of the intellect must be prompted by immediate action, paying no attention to those who stubbornly believe that reason is immutable. Definitive proof of that possibility is the practice of science, in accordance with the methodological reforms mentioned before, as well as the success of the results obtained. That science is always subject to revision has become widely accepted since the end of the last century. Having gained greater clarity of its means and ends, namely that it is a critique of knowledge directed at the reform of method, it has won new victories. For example, phenomenology, apart from its theoretical commitments, has developed a method that has been fruitfully applied in different areas of the specialized sciences.

---

9. [Husserl's *Logical Investigations* was translated into Spanish by Manuel García Morente and José Gaos. It was published in 1929 in the *Revista de Occidente*.]

CHAPTER THREE

Theory of Objects

One aspiration of human knowledge is to reduce the diversity of reality to the unity of a concept. However, to achieve this non-artificially, reality must allow for it by imposing on knowledge a structure that is identical everywhere and that changes only in its external, apparent manifestation. Now, this is what intellectualism has always proposed as the basis of its speculations and the idea guiding its methods. If we suppose, for example, that psychic reality is, at its root, identical to physical reality and varies only in appearance, it makes sense that one try to use the same methods to explore the psychic and the physical, and the same principles to explain both. If this ontological assumption were true, there would be only one method for all sciences and only one system of categories for every sphere of reality. This would imply that the very same system of laws governs every class of beings and events in the universe. As it happens, the particular sciences shared this point of view toward the end of the last century and, as a result, the methods and principles taken from physics were applied exclusively and in the same way to biology, as well as to psychology and sociology.[1] The intellectualist philosophy of the same period affirmed the same scientific attitude.

One must acknowledge that the concept of a unified reality was a simplistic hypothesis, a completely unfounded assumption of logic. On the contrary, direct intuition of reality reveals that there are ontological regions that vary in structure. To be convinced of this, one need only eliminate all preconceived ideas, every scientific and philosophical theory, and put oneself in direct contact with authentic

---

1. [Ramos seems to be referring to what was called "intertheoretic reduction." A famous example was Ludwig Edward Boltzmann's attempt to reduce thermodynamics into statistical mechanics in the nineteenth century.]

reality, as it presents itself to intuition. Almost every great philosopher of our time has fought to establish this truth. It is not a matter of substituting one hypothesis for another, since the idea that reality is multiplicitous is a plain fact of experience. Whoever approaches reality as it is with an attitude of primitive ingenuousness will perceive that there is an enormous difference between a physical and a psychic fact, and that they represent two modes of being that seem to be dissimilar in every way. Reality will be understood only if it is divided into regions, each one of which corresponds to what Husserl calls a "regional ontology."

What, then, are these ontological regions? For the time being, and so long as research does not discover new ones, modern theory admits of four. These four regions are the following: (1) that of real objects, which include three layers: (a) physical-chemical facts, (b) biological facts, (c) psychological facts; (2) ideal objects that are divided into (a) relations, (b) mathematical objects, (c) essences; (3) the world of values; (4) human existence.

The study and knowledge of each of these objects requires its own logic, composed of a set of categories and methods specific to the region. To that end, what is needed is a reform of the intellect that, until recently mainly proved adequate for comprehending physical facts.[2] Bergson says that the intellect is essentially geometric; it has been formed through its encounter with inorganic material and it naturally misunderstands life. I do not mean to suggest that the intellect is reformed before it is applied in a determinate ontological region. Reform is possible only once the intellect takes effect in a sphere of reality, from which it should extract categories that are adequate for understanding said sphere. What belongs to the objects in and of themselves is designated by the term *ontic*. And what belongs to the logic specific to each object is called ontological.

Of these regions I will focus on the fourth, that is, on human existence, which is the most independent of them all and through

---

2. [Ortega y Gasset uses the expression "reforma de la inteligencia" in *Mission of the University*, trans. Howard Lee Nostrand (New York: Routledge, 1946).]

which the others intersect. By human existence I do not mean, as has already been explained, only the existence of a human subject, but, at the same time, the existence of real and ideal objects, as well as of values, as they directly relate to it. Human existence, then, consists of the human being and their world, and therefore the other three ontological categories are included and refer to human existence. Only by including within "human existence" both the subject and object is it possible to overcome the antithesis between idealism and realism.

This research today is represented by a cutting-edge mode of thought that has been called "existential philosophy," whose main shortcoming is, for the moment, that of not having established adequate *a priori* principles. Distinguished contemporary philosophers have paved the way for this new field which is barely in its initial phase. The most outstanding trailblazers of this new continent include: in France, Boutroux and Bergson; in Germany, Scheler, Hartmann, and Heidegger; and in Spain, Ortega y Gasset and García Morente.

Boutroux and Bergson are not typically included on this list, but reading Boutroux's *The Contingency of the Laws of Nature* and almost everything Bergson has written allows us to find valuable ideas and suggestions for existential philosophy. *[Time and Free Will:] An Essay on the Immediate Data of Consciousness* presents a brilliant case in which Bergson demonstrates the error psycho-physics makes in applying the categories of the material world, especially the notion of space, to the understanding of the world of the soul. That error prevented us from understanding the true nature of psychic life, and thereby distorted our understanding of human personality and freedom. In *Creative Evolution*, Bergson has demonstrated the limit of rational knowledge, how it misunderstands life, and he defended the thesis of the reform of intellect. The concepts of life, time, consciousness, freedom, etc., reappear today as dominant themes in existential philosophy. It is only fair, then, to give Bergson the credit he deserves as a precursor of this philosophical movement.

Bibliography[3]

Descartes, René. *Meditations on First Philosophy.*

Hartmann, Nicolai. *Metaphysik der Erkenntnis* [Metaphysics of Knowledge], *Sistematische Selbstdarstellung* [Systematic Self-Exposure], *Zum Problem der Realitätsgegebenheit* [On the Problem of the Givenness of Reality].[4]

Bergson, Henri. *Creative Evolution.*

Husserl, Edmund. *Ideas para una fenomenología, etc.* (trans. Esp., FCE, México, 1962) [Ideas: General Introduction to Pure Phenomenology].

Ortega y Gasset, José. *Meditations on Quixote. The Modern Theme.*

Windelband, Wilhem. *Preludes.*

García Morente, Manuel. *Lecciones preliminares de filosofía*, Universidad de Tucumán, 1938 [Preliminary Lessons of Philosophy].

---

3. [This short bibliography is in Ramos's original text. We have substituted the English titles where possible.]

4. [Nicolai Hartmann, *Ontology: Laying the Foundations*, trans. Keith Peterson (Berlin: De Gruyter, 2019).]

CHAPTER FOUR
Agenda for a Philosophical Anthropology

I want to inform the reader that I have ventured to write these pages, not with the intention of laying out an original theory of the human being, but as part of the more modest effort to outline a philosophical itinerary through a new area of study rarely systematized. This essay, then, limits itself to defining the fundamental problems of philosophical anthropology and unifying its ideas in an exposition that responds more adequately to these problems. It takes as its subject a brand-new branch of philosophy and, therefore, it would be unfair to ask it to provide definitive conclusions. It is still in the early stages of development, and it should be used to introduce its problems methodically and secure its epistemological foundation, which should help to solve them with philosophical rigor.

The theories of every great philosopher, going back to the Greeks, contain ideas concerning the human; what is more, I believe that every major turn of thought implies a conception of the human being. Moreover, almost every philosophical discipline is occupied by some particular aspect of human activity, knowledge, morality, art, etc., and the same applies to some of the positive sciences. That is why it is especially important that philosophical anthropology has recently been established as a discipline apart from the others. This fact alone reveals that human existence has been recognized as a peculiar and irreducible object. The birth of this discipline corresponds to the emergence of a new awareness of human life that is not satisfied with understanding itself in sections or fragments, but which discovers itself as a coherent whole that can be studied only as such in order to understand what it is. Anthropology, then, is not a synthesis of knowledge taken from different sciences, but an independent field of knowledge that corresponds directly to its object and that, with the ideas it obtains, should provide the other sciences guidance concerning their bodies of knowledge. This is to say that philosophical anthropology is a fundamental and basic science, and that the conclusions of the sciences that study partial aspects of human beings ought to be interpreted through its principles. Since the other sciences existed before, once anthropology determines its fundamental principles, scientific theories that have developed without any guiding conception of the human must be revised.

Before adopting just any dogmatic position, before adhering to this or that anthropological theory, the fundamental task of philosophical anthropology is to analyze what is essential in the way we think about the human being. So, the object of this first inquiry is not the reality of being human, but rather our ideal representation of it. This initial phase of the inquiry, then, tries to define the essence of the human being *a priori*, that is, to define a set of features that we cannot logically separate from the general idea of the human and whose justification does not require the confirmation of reality or empirical verification. This phase amounts to a phenomenology of the human aligned with the method established by Husserl.

In our time, Martin Heidegger, adhering to Husserl's method, introduced a phenomenology of human existence, but he did so in language so abstruse that it hinders an adequate understanding and appreciation of its results. Naturally, outside phenomenology, before Husserl and Heidegger, many thinkers have contributed valuable intuitions concerning the conceptions of the human, not to mention details scattered throughout classical philosophy and even the positive sciences. If we were to review these contributions and included those that satisfy strictly phenomenological criteria, we might assemble a large portion of the material needed to establish the fundamental principles of philosophical anthropology. But if we confine ourselves to the thinkers near us, we find valuable contributions to this new science in Boutroux, Bergson, Scheler, Hartmann, and Ortega y Gasset. Scheler ought to be cited apart as a thinker who dedicated himself to developing philosophical anthropology and to whom we owe books like *The Human Place in the Cosmos*, the best breviary on the subject, as well as studies that appear in his other works and freestanding essays.

Among the ideas concerning the human, we have to pick out a basic set of ideas supported by the strongest evidence in order to establish the axioms of anthropology. Precisely because they are axiomatic, some of these ideas might seem banal or obvious, truths that everyone already knows, and one might ask why the philosopher exerts so much energy to establish what is already known. Such is the case with some of Heidegger's most innovative theses, which, stripped of their philosophical terminology and expressed in common language, appear to lose their claim to novelty. Nevertheless, doing so is not mere pedantry, or a useless endeavor, since the fact that a notion is already known is not a justification of its truth. It is essential to discover it by means of methodical reflection in order to confer philosophical validity upon it, and we should not be surprised by its banality, since, as Descartes demonstrated, clear ideas are precisely the simplest.

True, these ideas teach us little to nothing, since generally they are analytical judgments that only express an idea already contained in the concept to be clarified. The absolute certainty of these judgments stems from the fact that they adhere strictly to the logical principle of identity, even though, conversely, they appear to be tautologically true. Naturally, these truths on their own do not constitute a complete science of the human being; if they did, it would be extremely impoverished and insufficient. The value of these ideas appears only if they are considered a starting point, the assumptions or categories of anthropological knowledge. The phenomenology of human existence, on its own, cannot be the totality of philosophical anthropology. Once the essence of the human being is defined *a priori*, it is necessary to begin constructing the science in the strict sense and to confront the empirical reality of humans and the theories about them that have been disseminated.

Axioms of Human Ontology

Human life is not mere existing, as is the case with the things that surround it, but, and this is important, it is also knowing that it exists. Human existence is distinguished from all other forms of existence in that it is aware of its existence. A rock, an insect, and a tree exist, but they do not know it. Consciousness is, so to speak, a revelation of being. Now, consciousness is not an "epiphenomenon," a mere aggregate that accompanies existence in order to keep track of it; it is not a reflecting surface intended for contemplation. Consciousness gives human existence its peculiar mode of being; it is inseparable from its ontological structure. When I become aware of my existence, I am not aware of it alone, as if in a vacuum, but on the contrary my existence is given to me situated among a set of facts that influence and that at the same time are the aim of my action. Consciousness, then, makes me feel like one existence among others, occupying a certain place among them. In Heidegger's parlance, the basic trait of human existence is "being-in-the-world." Furthermore, I do not feel like a fixed existence, immobile, but like something that is constantly flowing. I am not only conscious of my current state, of the "here" and "now" alone, but I also have memories and expectations. I can recall my prior states, what has already happened, and through representation I also anticipate what has yet to come. In a word, I have intentions, projects, and hopes.

I call consciousness precisely the capacity to hold on to images of the past and project my imagination toward the future. But these acts, which I am separating in this exposition because one cannot discuss everything all at once, are actually interwoven in the living present, enriching its content and forming an uninterrupted continuum that constitutes time. Consciousness, then, gives human existence its temporal dimension. All other external things that make up our world also appear to us in time even though time does not exist for them. By contrast, time is with us; our existence *is* time. The concept of time, then, has two meanings, depending on whether we apply it to the external world or to our own lives. In the first case, time is not a reality, properly speaking, but merely a relation that characterizes things as they flow through the channel of our sensibility. In the case of our lives, however, time is not the channel but the river itself that runs through the channel. In the latter case, time has ontic reality; it is an integral part of human existence.

Like other living beings, the human is a process constantly unfolding. In the plant and animal worlds, however, this process invariably follows the same curve, each species in accordance with an archetype, which the individual reproduces exactly. In other words, all those beings have a predetermined destiny that is governed in every detail by an inevitable law. Human existence also has its share of inevitability. At its root, human existence appears to be a project aimed at its own survival. Each person must first concern themselves with making their own way, which requires them to think in terms of the future, to imagine with anticipation what will be. That is why Ortega says that the human is essentially a "preoccupied" being.[1] First and foremost, one has to live. We encounter life as an urgent problem to be resolved. The preservation of existence is pressed upon us as an inescapable necessity, and life itself as a constant risk, the risk of being lost. The possibility of death emerges and is the source of anxiety that is a feature of human existence to varying degrees.

The uncertainty of human life indicates that it is not entirely predetermined. Largely determined, life contains a margin of freedom. The human being is full of possibilities and has a variable capacity to choose among them; we can voluntarily propose an end and complete it. The basic principle of human life is not reduced to the mere conservation and preservation of existence. If animal life is a vicious circle, appearing as a tendency that starts with life in order to return to it, human life can search for meaning that transcends mere living and that represents, in addition to survival, an enrichment of life. But we will return to this point later. For now, we will only conclude by saying that in the region of being, the human appears as a teleological entity, one that consciously proposes goals to oneself and tries to achieve them. This characteristic trait resides only in the human because it is provided by knowledge and foresight. Whereas animal existence is dot-like, a discontinuous process of present moments, human existence is amplified into continuous becoming that goes from the past to the future through the present. Memory is the organ of the past; foresight, of the future.

---

1. [See, for example, José Ortega y Gasset, *What Is Philosophy?*]

The Human Being as "Ought to Be"

Human life, as we previously stated, is not one abstract event distinct from the rest, but is tethered existentially to the world. But what is the world? For humans, before they possess rational knowledge of it, the world is a set of pressures and resistances that hinder the free development of the vital impulse. For this reason, life acquires the character of a conflict between a being and its environment, which, depending on one's opportunities, might resolve itself in success or failure. Different elements intersect in that environment but can ultimately be reduced to two: nature and society. Life is an endless fight to survive, but not everything that surrounds it is hostile; on the contrary, there are multiple paths that are already mapped out beforehand, preestablished frameworks that foster the formation and development of life. If on the one hand the environment is a constraint on liberty, in exchange it supports and facilitates labor. The ontology of human existence cannot ignore the fact that humans are "political animals," beings that live in society. Out of necessity, every individual must situate their life within the civilizing frameworks that society has created. Human life implicitly takes up the task of harmonizing individual will with the general demands of civilization.

Kant once said that the human being is a "citizen of two worlds," alluding to another important fact of human existence. The human is a moral being, that is, a being that faces demands and duties of an ideal nature. Human consciousness is not only consciousness of what is, but also of what "ought to be," which is like a bridge that leads humans from the world of facts to the world of values. In this last sense, Kant's phrase is accurate. The world of facts and the world of values are not separate worlds. In our own lives and the reality that surrounds us, some things are valuable; others are devoid of value. The ways in which we value things enable us to envision how imperfect things ought to be. The world of values, therefore, is an ideal projection of how things ought to be. Values constitute the goal of all human action. When we propose an end to ourselves, it is because we consider it valuable. One cannot say that they intentionally pursued an end that they believed had no value. This only happens when a person errors or is blind. We are now able to complete a proposition, mentioned earlier, that the human is a being that pursues valuable ends.

When reflecting on the essence of the human being we must not forget, even for a moment, that the human is never a static being, finished, but rather is an infinite process of constant becoming that unfolds in history. Animals and plants never cease to realize their essence and cannot but live as animals and plants. The many possibilities that appear on the horizon of human life make one's destiny uncertain. Humans can pursue ends that are not characteristically human; we can drift or veer off the path of our destiny. Destiny is something that we must discover. This is the great metaphysical problem of human existence. Natural science studies humans as they are, analyzes what we are made of, but without giving value to the ingredients. Science refrains from stating whether the characteristically human is rooted in such and such element of the compound. But we now realize that in order to define the essence of the human being, the fundamental problem of philosophical anthropology, it is necessary to move toward a metaphysics of the human that tells us how we ought to be. This raises a question of values that distinguishes this investigation from the point of view of the natural sciences. The human must be understood in terms of the values that serve as the ends of our activities. Given this essential relation between the human and values it is understood that the most important discoveries in this new discipline emerge from the field of ethics (Scheler, Hartmann).

Without trying to determine for the moment which value or set of values we ought to choose as the norm of behavior (an ethical problem), the general fact remains that human life is a constant inclination toward valuable ends. More technically: the human is an axiological entity. An essential feature of human nature is that there must be a direction that gives it meaning, a purpose that justifies it. The human in the full sense of the term always lives for something or because of something. A representative manifestation of this requirement is culture. Culture, as Scheler saw very well, is just the process of *humanization* that radiates from humans and is extended to the nature that surrounds them.² Out of a piece of stone, whose natural state lacks meaning and purpose, we produce an instrument or sculpture and change the stone into an object of culture. That fragment of nature now represents a human purpose—utility or beauty—which manifests the spirit of its creator. That inanimate object not only acquires value, but the person who produces such objects also captures a new value by their act of creation. What is natural in the human finds a meaning that elevates it to a higher plane. In culture, therefore, humans find the aim they require for existence. And that aim consists of creating oneself, in enriching one's life with new values at every step. What we call *spirit* is that capacity of making things or oneself an object of value.

Theories of the Human Being and the Arc of Humanism

Greek metaphysics exhibited a heightened propensity for anthropomorphizing, conceiving of the universe in terms of the human being, as the great animistic and teleological system of Aristotle demonstrates. By contrast, in modern philosophy, influenced by natural science, we tend to conceive of ourselves in terms of nature. That is, whereas the Greeks elevated nature to the level of the human in their theoretical pursuits, the moderns have lowered human beings to the level of nature. Only Christian philosophy locates human beings high above nature, attributing a religious, supernatural meaning to us. Contemporary philosophers have denounced these errors of perspective, having discovered that reality is divided into ontological regions that are diverse in structure. Philosophy will not make the mistake of explaining nature from the anthropomorphic point of view or *vice versa*. Its aspiration now is to explain each region, not from the outside, but from within using its own categories. The problem of

---

2. [Ramos is likely referring to Max Scheler's essay, "The Forms of Knowledge and Culture." See "Max Scheler" in this volume. See also Max Scheler, "Love and Knowledge," in *On Feeling, Knowing and Value: Selected Writings*, trans. H. J. Bershady with assistance of P. Haley (Chicago and London: The University of Chicago Press, 1992).]

philosophical anthropology stems from the fact that the human is an intersection in which various categories of being converge. But in which of these categories does the essence of the human consist? There are almost as many conceptions of the human as there are elements that constitute our existence. Each of these conceptions takes a part and tries to turn it into the whole of human existence, which is mutilated by a one-sidedness of vision. The human is conceived of in terms of reason, as will, as feeling, as instinct, etc. These notions stem from three sources: religion, philosophy, and natural science. Max Scheler has reduced these many conceptions to five types, each one of which has a corresponding philosophy of history.

I. The first is the Christian conception of the human being. Its origin is explained by the myth of creation and the first couple. Later came the doctrine of sin and redemption. The doctrine of an immortal soul, resurrection, and final judgment. The conception of history that corresponds to this idea is that of St. Augustine, as it is defined in *The City of God*.

II. The Greek conception of the human as *logos*, *ratio*, was turned into the concept of *homo sapiens*. Almost all anthropology, specifically the philosophical variety from Aristotle to Kant and Hegel, has adopted this conception, and in Western Europe it has the character of being a self-evident truth, even though, according to Scheler, it is only "an invention of the Greeks." The corresponding philosophy of history is Hegel's idealism.

III. This group includes a set of modern theories, largely developed by natural science, and to which we can refer using the Bergsonian phrase *homo faber*. According to these theories, the human is essentially an instinctual being. In line with the three classes of basic instincts we can distinguish three conceptions of the human, as represented by the instinct that outweighs the other two: (a) the *sexual* being; (b) the *powerful* being; (c) the *economic* being. To each of these three conceptions corresponds a theory of history: (a) the dominant historical factor is *blood* ([Joseph Arthur de] Gobineau, [Gustav] Ratzenhofer, [Ludwig] Gumplowitcz) and sexual instinct (Schopenhauer, Freud); (b) the theory of political power (Hobbes, Machiavelli, Nietzsche, [Alfred] Adler); and (c) the economic conception of history (Marx).

IV. At this point we arrive at a theory that Scheler believes is discordant, a misguided idea not accepted by the educated world, but which might very well be true: pessimistic ideologies of very different shades that regard the human as an animal in decline, as a sickness of life, as a species on its way to extinction. Researchers with widely different backgrounds representing distinct sciences agree on the results, including doctors, psychologists, ethnologists, philosophers, etc. It is almost exclusively a German idea. Its representatives include [Ludwig] Klages, [Ernest] Daqué, [Leo] Froebenius, [Oswald] Spengler, [Theodore] Lessing, etc.

V. The last conception mentioned by Scheler includes theories of the human that, rather than devalue us, exalt us to a height without precedent in history. This group includes [Dietrich Heinrich] Kerler, Scheler himself, and Nicolai Hartmann.[3]

The conceptions of the human outline various arcs throughout history, with alternative ascents and declines whose extreme degrees I will highlight next. From the moment of equilibrium that characterizes the Greek conception, human values take flight and culminate in the Christian idea that attributes a supernatural rank to the human being. Renaissance humanism was a movement to bring human values from heaven back to earth. If the arc from Greece to the Middle Ages ascends, the Renaissance initiated a descending turn. Humanism limited itself to returning the conception of the human and human values to the level of equilibrium that the Greeks had left it at. Modern natural science then took human values and lowered them to the point of making them distinctly infrahuman. It is here that the arc begins an upward flight emphasizing the very recent effort of philosophy to rescue human values and put them in their proper place. We can call this last effort a *New Humanism* whose direction is upward from below, as opposed to Renaissance humanism, which aimed in the opposite direction. Moreover, Renaissance humanism was simply a flight back to the classical Greek conception, whereas the new

---

3. [For these five conceptions of the human being, see Max Scheler, "Man and History," in *Philosophical Perspectives*, trans. Oscar Haac (Boston: Beacon Press, 1958 [1926]).]

humanism is more fully aware, much better informed, of the values peculiar to the human being and of their cosmic relations.

We do not completely disregard the value of observing the human being. Without question, because of science, we possess a knowledge of human life more profound and complete than ever before. We now know quite a bit concerning the natural dimension of the human being [*el hombre-naturaleza*]. However, science proceeds by abstraction, dissecting human life into parts: physical life, psychological life, social life, juridical life, etc. But the aspiration of philosophical anthropology is to obtain a conception of the human being as a totality. The repertory of diverse historical conceptions of the human corresponds to a series of empirical types, limited in number, none of which represents the totality of humankind. Therefore, it makes sense that anthropology aspires to arrive at a supra-historical and supra-empirical conception of the human that retains only those elements that apply to everyone independently of their temporal location or empirical particularities. If the human is a composite of diverse elements, anthropology does not privilege one at the expense of the others. Anthropology accepts every element with the rights that belong to each, since the problem of anthropology is to determine how these specific elements are integrated into a whole, how they relate to one another and what their essential structure is. Anthropology inquires whether it is possible to order these elements on a hierarchy or according to an objective scale of values.

A New Appraisal of Instincts

Through the experience of one's neighbor, natural science studies the human from the outside, as a biological being, a psychological being, a social being, etc. Among the most valuable conclusions that science has obtained using this method are those pertaining to our psycho-biological constitution. Psychoanalytic schools have increased our knowledge of the mechanisms of the psyche considerably, exploring what has been until very recently terra incognita: the unconscious. Because of its findings, we better understand the role of different instincts in human life. We ought to acknowledge that this psychological knowledge, interpreted through the philosophy of life (Dilthey, Nietzsche, Bergson, Ortega), has led to a new appraisal of instincts. Many centuries of a religious and philosophical culture, skewed to one side in favor of spiritual values, held a moral prejudice against the instinctual—namely, it was considered an impurity in the human, a malign force opposed to all superior design. Progress in culture was thought possible only through the annihilation and expulsion of all instinctual influence in the scope of life. Nowadays, this problem is judged using a different criterion and the values of the body, which is the organ of the instincts, tend to reclaim their legitimate rights.

But this in no way is meant to defend naturalists who reduce all of our activity to instinct. According to such theories, even the higher functions involving consciousness can be explained by unconscious motives. When one believes that consciousness acts in response to moral, aesthetic, and logical values, etc., one overlooks that in reality the true motives are sexual, economic, or related to power. Consciousness, then, is always deceived, as if it were destined to turn truth into illusion. It could be argued that the purpose of consciousness is to enlighten instinct, to guide its pursuits toward their best possible fulfillment. But we know by observing animal life that instinct does not require consciousness at all, that the more blind it is, the more successful it is in achieving its ends. Consciousness is an "epiphenomenon" or a complication of life that justifies the theory according to which humans, given their intellectual life, take the long route to obtain what the animal, guided by pure instinct, procures easily. The error in theories of instinct is that they exaggerate the role of the unconscious and overlook the autonomy of conscious life.

To prove naturalist theories of the human being, science would have to show clearly that the higher orders of being can be explained by the lower. That said, in the nineteenth century this idea was scientific dogma that became a methodological norm. Biology was explained by physical-chemical laws; psychology, by biological laws, and so on. This method was based on the assumption—mentioned often in this exposition—and thus was submitted as proof, that very different natural phenomena are at bottom identical. This identity of what is real promised that every order of nature could eventually be explained by the same principle. The so-called "theory of objects" in philosophy, in connection with the development of the sciences, has discovered the inconsistency of that hypothesis. In this century, the sciences have begun to be divided into autonomous disciplines that explain their respective objects each with their own principles. In accordance with this new course of the special sciences, philosophy developed a new theory of "categories" and "regional ontologies." No longer accepted today, the system that explains a category of being by the one just below it was possible only because of a stratagem that consisted in presupposing below the existence of what is to be explained above. For example, how can one infer the consciousness of the organic without assuming that it already exists at least latently? Boutroux says:

> In reality, what we are here analyzing under the name of consciousness is not consciousness itself, but either its condition or its object. Its conditions form a complex whole, reducible, it may be, either wholly or partially, to physiological and physical elements. Similarly, its object (sensations, thoughts, desires), considered in itself, forms a complex whole, which may offer a more or less exact parallelism to the succession of physiological facts. Consciousness itself, however, is an irreducible datum which explanation obscures and analysis destroys. To try to find the detailed elements of consciousness for the purpose of contrasting or connecting them with the elements of the lower functions, is to lose sight of consciousnesses itself and to consider its materials or its products.... [Consciousness] is a new element, a new creation. Man, endowed with consciousness as he is, is more than a living being.[4]

According to Boutroux, the universe of which the human being is a part is not a uniform ensemble, as science supposes, but a totality composed of strata or layers of diverse existential content, which, though some are supported by others, possess a mode of being that is peculiar and autonomous: it is a pluralistic universe constituted by

---

4. [Emile Boutroux, *The Contingency of Laws of Nature*, trans. Fred Rothwell (Chicago and London: Open Court Publishing, 1916), 115–17.]

various worlds that are staggered like floors of a building. Boutroux writes:

> Each of these worlds appears, at first, to depend strictly on the lower worlds, as on some external fatality, and to receive from them its existence and laws. Would matter exist without generic identity and causality, bodies without matter, living beings without physical agents, man without life?
>
> Nevertheless, if we examine and compare the concepts of the principle forms of being, we see that it is impossible to connect the higher forms with the lower ones by a link of necessity.... We cannot deduce the higher forms from the lower by way of analysis because the higher contain elements that cannot be reduced to those of the lower. The first find in the second only their matter, not their form.[5]

According to this theory, it should be understood that, among the various layers of being, there is a relative dependence and a relative independence. The highest layer cannot exist without the lowest. Thought can only appear given that certain vital conditions are met. These conditions feed or support its existence. But then, on top of this base, the development of thought takes flight, and thought can choose its own ends, which purely vital conditions do not fully explain. By contrast, the inferior strata can exist without the superior. To a certain extent, humans can develop their pure animality without trying or without the help of the spirit. Nicolai Hartmann has deduced from these facts laws that determine the precise relation of dependence and independence of the categories. To the extent that the superior strata depend on the inferior for their existence, they are clearly weaker. Thus, in this order, the spirit is the weaker category of being, that of inanimate material is the stronger. In the universe, the physical world is wholly indifferent to living beings and moves with fearsome strength. For their part, biological laws act like a force that does not factor in nobler pursuits. This hierarchy of strength does not in any way change the objective hierarchy of values, which are structured the other way around. Despite their weakness, moral acts,

---

5. [Boutroux, *Contingency*, 152.]

aesthetic contemplation, or a scientific or a philosophical idea continue to be more valuable than brute strength. Except for the material world at the base of the system, every stratum of being needs an inferior stratum merely to exist. Once it exists, its actions are governed by independent laws. In the universe, therefore, there is no uniform system of laws but different types of law that run parallel to the strata of being. It would be extraordinarily fruitful to revise the philosophical interpretations of history, both those that explain history only from below and those that explain it from above, in order to expose their falsity and to make urgent the need for a different assessment from the point of view of new anthropological knowledge.

The Layers of the Human Being

These relations of categories allow us to better understand the articulation and the coordinated functioning of the different layers of the human being. But first, philosophical anthropology should determine exactly what layers there are. It should lay out the essential structure of the human being, whose schema is universally valid, and which can be thought of as the template used to list individual or group variations whose origins are historical, racial, cultural, etc.

The religious and philosophical tradition has conceived of the human dualistically. For Plato, Aristotle, and Greek philosophy the distinction between mind and body represents a dualism that is both ontological and moral. Implicit in the concepts of mind and body are judgments of value that create a metaphysical opposition between good and evil. In the modern period, Descartes was the first to recognize this dualist conception and take it to a radical extreme, deepening the metaphysical division between mind and body. The prejudice of dualism is so widespread that natural science also divides the human being into two and studies biology, on the one hand, and psychology on the other. Even though the concepts of mind and body correspond in metaphysics to immaterial being and animal being, there is a certain imprecision in what each of these concepts encompasses, and what each refers to varies over time and different theories. Almost every major position in metaphysics reflects a dualist conception of human being: mechanism and finalism, freedom and necessity, etc. If this classic schema reproduces two of the most dominant faces of the human being, it does not entirely square with their true structure as it appears under a more rigorous observation of the facts. Ortega y Gasset offered a fuller and more accurate view of the architecture of the human being by distinguishing three fundamental layers, which he called Vitality, Soul, and Spirit. Ortega's philosophical hypothesis does not trade in artificial distinctions, but provides a description that sticks to what is directly observed in the phenomena.[6]

The base or foundation of the entire human person is, for Ortega, the "soul embodied" or "Vitality," which includes the instincts of offense and defense, of power and play, organic sensations, pleasure and pain, sexual attraction, sensitivity to rhythm. This is the base of the somatic and the psychological, the corporeal and the spiritual, and not only are they blended here but it is from here that they originate and are nourished. Each human has a vital force that overflows or is deficient, healthy or sick, and the degree of vitality largely depends on one's character. Vitality corresponds to a kind of "intrabody," the body as everyone perceives it from within. The intrabody is constituted by the set of all internal sensations: of movement, of touch, of the viscera, muscles, joints, arteries, etc. This notion corresponds almost exactly to what in psychophysiology is called "cenesthesia." Since cenesthesia is always present, it is almost unconscious, except in pathological cases such as, for example, certain states of neurasthenia. The entire scope of sensuality belongs to the intrabody. There are human beings who live primarily from their vitality or who are pure vitality, such as children and savages. When vitality is active, we place ourselves outside the center of our person. In moments of play, in sport, in sensual life, the individual forgets oneself and blends with the rest of nature.

Human personality is nourished from the treasure of vitality. If we go further in from this peripheral zone of the body, we encounter two separate regions: the soul and the spirit. The reason we must distinguish the soul and spirit is that in our interior we perceive certain

---

6. [See José Ortega y Gasset, "Vitalidad, alma, espíritu," in *Obras completas*, vol. 2: El Espectador (1916–1934) (Madrid: Revista de Occidente, 1963).]

movements that are not prompted by our own will, those which we do not feel like we are the author of. Emotions, feelings, passions, sympathies, antipathies are awakened in us without our assent and, even though they are in us, they are produced in spite of oneself. We would rather not have them, but nevertheless we do. They are *my* feelings, but they are not *me*, because I do not identify with them. Here we find romantic passion and, more generally, the life of feeling, that is, the private world of individual life. The movements of the soul can be repressed or set free by other forces over which our person has control. The spirit is the center of the person, the "set of private acts about which each person believes themselves to be the author or main character."[7] The spirit is made up of will and thought. It constitutes what we call, strictly speaking, the *self*. The self is the central point of our person that resolves and decides; it is what in the act of understanding and knowing is put in direct contact with what is known.

There is another difference between the soul and spirit: spiritual phenomena do not endure, but those of the soul occur over time. We might take a long time to come to understand something, but the understanding itself is the work of an instant; similarly, preparing for an act might take long, but one makes the decision to act in a moment. By contrast, everything that belongs to the soul is developed in time. "One is sad or happy for a time—for a day or for one's whole life."[8]

The spirit is the center of the person; however, it is governed by impersonal norms. In order to think the truth, one must abide by the norms of logic and adjust the intellect to the being of things. For that reason, pure thought is the same in all individuals and everyone thinks the same way when they are thinking. The will also operates according to objective norms, what ought to be, values. Consequently, the soul is the realm of subjectivity; the spirit, the realm of objectivity.

---

7. [Ortega y Gasset, "Vitalidad, alma, espíritu," 461.]

8. [Ortega y Gasset, "Vitalidad, alma, espíritu," 462.]

It should be understood that the notion of the spirit does not correspond to the traditional concept of a metaphysical entity hidden behind phenomena. What we affirm about the spirit is fully justified by experience, from which such affirmations have been deduced. Even though we can no longer accept the old metaphysical theories of the spirit, direct observation of phenomena presents us with a set of peculiarly human activities that, because they cannot be reduced to other activities, deserve to be called human. Evidently the intelligence, will, intuition of values, are functions that are not governed by psychophysical laws. Scheler defines the spirit as "objectivity" or "the possibility of being determined by the objects themselves." Spirit, then, is the life of the subject that transcends its individuality in order to seek its law in the objective world, whether real or ideal. The spirit is a direction of human life that is personal at the start but whose goal is the supra-individual. This should not be interpreted to mean that the spirit exists as something universal outside the individual. The spirit exists only in the singular concentration that we call a "person." We live with the spirit in the moments in which we do not live for ourselves as individuals. There are two possible forms of life: in one we live as isolated beings, in the other we live with the world. The latter represents spiritual life. Ortega says, "What does seem to be clear is that when we think or desire, we abandon our individuality and begin to participate in a universal sphere, where other spirits come out to participate as ours does. So that even though it is the most personal that there is in us—if by 'person' we understand the origin of one's own actions—the spirit strictly speaking does not live on its own but through the True, through the Norm, etc., etc.; it lives through an objective world in which it is supported, from which it receives its characteristic structure [*contextura*]. Said differently: the spirit does not rest in itself, but is rooted and based in that universal and transubjective sphere. A spirit that functions by itself and before itself, according to its manner, taste, and temper is not a spirit but a soul."[9]

---

9. [Ortega y Gasset, "Vitalidad, alma, espíritu," 466–67.]

CHAPTER FIVE

Objectivity of Values

Preliminary Remarks

Human beings always act in accordance with the ends that they deem valuable, and they never, except unconsciously, prefer what is worse over what is better. The key to understanding someone's specific psychology is to be found in their peculiar consciousness of values, that is, how they rank the things—as possible objects of their will—they value. The world presents us with many objects of interest, be they objects of action, knowledge, utility, or artistic representation, etc. Each interest presents the will with an ideal trajectory that shines before human consciousness with greater or lesser value. Each historical epoch has an ideal table of values from which one derives norms for the improvement of their life. In our epoch, we are witnessing a crisis of values. It would be risky [*aventurado*] to claim that any one scale of values is universally accepted. It seems better to say that concerning the hierarchy of values, there is no consensus, and that confusion and chaos reign. Certain widespread theories have even gone so far as to deny the very foundations of values. It has been said that values are merely subjective appraisals that only make sense to the person making the judgment. As such, there is no common denominator whatsoever to measure with objective certainty the Beautiful, the Good, the True—in short, all the qualities that make up the content of human culture. In this way, the world of values is reduced to pure illusion, without laws, wherein the only arbiter is individual whim. Subjectivism [*el subjetivo*][1] is the philosophical justification of this form of anarchy, affirming the principle of *homo mensura* as the

---

1. [It is not clear here whether Ramos is referring to "subjectivism," understood as a philosophical position, as the sentence suggests, or to "the subjective," understood as the substantive form of "subjectivity."]

only truth, which is expressed in the following formula: each individual is the measure of all things.

Nietzsche was the first to lend philosophical rigor to moral subjectivism. The value of life rests on a decision of the will. Only one who affirms life finds it valuable. In this way, value is a consequence of a stance one has already taken, not the other way around, as one might suppose. However, given his insistence on discussing these themes, Nietzsche can also be credited with bringing philosophical attention to values.[2] One of the most important results of philosophy today is restoring the conviction that values are independent of the ever-changing subjective conditions of valuing. We can conceive of the world of culture as grounded in an order of values that also obeys strictly objective laws, as does the natural world. The author of this essay thinks that it is urgent to disseminate these ideas in Mexico, where skepticism and mistrust have prevailed for many years. In our country, the meaning of values has lacked fixed principles, having always been employed completely arbitrarily. Every effort to correct our vicious habits of judgment is thus beneficial, as it propagates the view that there are intrinsic values in human life that our consciousness might acknowledge or ignore but whose reality is inalterable and does not depend on our relative points of view.

Our judgments of values are very often influenced by subjective circumstances. This means that we confer value on things only as they relate to our interests. A desired object appears to be valuable, and its degree of value varies according to one's power to obtain it. The further out of reach something is, the more valuable it is, and its value decreases the easier it is to acquire. It is not uncommon that when one grabs ahold of a desired object, its value vanishes completely; its value was an illusion projected onto the object to draw us toward it more passionately. This is an undeniably real fact of psychology, but it should not be confused with true acts of valuing. Desire and value are independent of each other so that it is possible to value a thing

---

2. [See, for example, Friedrich Nietzsche, *The Gay Science*, trans. Walter Kaufmann (New York: Viking, 1974); *On the Genealogy of Morals*, trans. Maudemarie Clark and Alan Swensen (Indianapolis: Hackett Publishing Company, 1998); and *Beyond Good and Evil*, trans. Walter Kaufmann (New York: Viking, 1966).]

without desiring it and desire a thing without valuing it. In any case, when desire and value go together, the former follows the latter, not the other way around, as is mistakenly supposed.

Love, hate, envy, resentment, spite are all passions that strongly influence judgments of value. One praises the qualities of a person whom they love and attributes a reputation to them that they might not deserve. Conversely, someone's worth can be diminished entirely out of antipathy or enmity. People always deem false the values of a person they envy. When a coveted object is beyond someone's reach, however hard they try to obtain it, they disguise their impotence by minimizing the value of the object, like the fox in the fable that calls the grapes beyond its reach green.[3] These and other observations not mentioned demonstrate, not that values are subjective, but that there are vicious attitudes—attitudes that cause mistakes in valuing—which can be consciously eliminated in order to find a pure vision of authentic value.

But, the subjectivist objects, how is it possible to grant a common standard of values if what one finds good, another judges bad, if what is agreeable to one is disagreeable to another? Ortega y Gasset rightly observes that the subjectivist theory of value, as with similar theories, emerges from a predisposition native to the modern human being. "We are, in effect, born subjectivists. It is noteworthy to find the ease with which the common man of today accepts every thesis in which what appears to be objective is explained away as a mere subjective projection."[4] Philosophical subjectivism is an old idea, formulated by the Sophist Protagoras (fifth century, BC) in his famous phrase,

---

3. ["The Fox and the Grapes" is an Aesop fable, later retold by Phaedrus and Jean de La Fontaine, among others.]

4. *¿Qué son los valores?*, Revista de Occidente, octubre de 1923. See also M. Scheler, *El resentimiento en la moral*, where he explains how values become subjective by means of *resentment*, p. 193. [José Ortega y Gasset, "Introduction to an Estimative Science: What Are Values," trans. Carlos Alberto Sánchez, in *The New Yearbook of Phenomenology and Phenomenological Philosophy: Special Issue: Phenomenology in the Hispanic World*, ed. Antonio Zirión Quijano, Jethro Bravo González, Noé Expósito Ropero, and Jonathan Jehu Guereca Carreón (New York: Routledge, 2023), 125–39.]

"Man is the measure of all things." To accept this principle, whose original meaning was individualistic, would be to deny the existence of an objective order that is universally valid (be it moral, aesthetic, or another kind). Scheler says, "All modern theories of value share the premise that values as such, and moral values in particular, are only subjective phenomena in man's mind which have no independent meaning and existence. Values, according to this view, are but the projections of our desires and feelings. 'What is desired is good, what is abhorred is bad.' Reality as such, without human desires and emotions, is supposed to be entirely value-free."[5]

Undoubtedly, unless one is constantly on guard, one inserts a subjective point of view into their judgment of the value of things and people. But does it follow that nothing in reality has intrinsic value? In response to subjectivism's radical negation, we should examine the testimony of an unbiased consciousness. In the moments when the subject breaks free from oneself and opens their consciousness to the reality of things, they discover that behind the veil of apparent values, things possess other values inherent to their nature that cannot be changed by our wills. We cannot change the fact that an action is wrong or a painting is ugly through an act of will. There is a plane of objective values that does not depend on pleasure or desire. Pleasure is a value, but not all values are pleasurable. Things are not valuable because we desire them; we desire them because they are valuable. In every disinterested act of valuation, authentic values show themselves to consciousness. Only a small-minded spirit does not recognize the worth, if there be any, of what is contrary to its pleasure or desire. The person of profound moral and artistic consciousness lends credence to the fact that their judgment of value is dictated by the objects themselves, on account of certain independent qualities, in reality, not by the person who judges them.

---

5. [Max Scheler, *Ressentiment*, trans. Louis A. Coser (Milwaukee: Marquette University Press, 1994), 69.]

The World of Values

So far, we have discussed the existence of real values inherent in facts, persons, and things. But consciousness also discovers abstract values, detached from reality, in a pure state, so to speak. In the estimation of real objects, we do observe not only the values that they do possess but also the values that they *ought* to possess. Those gifted with a fine sensibility for value find reality imperfect and judge that it is not *as it ought to be*. Now, how is such judgment possible if one does not possess an ideal model with which to compare real facts? That model is nothing other than the model of pure values. Without pure values, we would not be able to undertake any valuing whatsoever. How would we recognize actual values in reality if we did not have a previous idea of what those ideal values are? A condition of all valuation, then, is the notion of pure values, which constitutes the necessary premise of all valid estimation. In this way, then, hovering above reality, which is always deficient, consciousness reveals a world of ideal values, in virtue of which we know what *ought to be*. This conception is neither more nor less than pure Platonism, with the sole difference that Plato spoke about Ideas and we are now speaking about Values. Hartmann says, "There is a kingdom of values that subsists unto itself, a genuine *kosmos noetos* (intelligible world) that exists beyond reality and beyond consciousness."[6] A positivistic prejudice, widely held, might prevent the recognition of a truth confirmed by experience—namely, that having a sense of ideal values is an authentic experience. Such is the case with values like justice, for example, which one can intuit as an idea even if it has never been fully actualized. This case also shows us that values are valuable regardless of whether they are carried out in concrete facts. Heroism would not lose one ounce of value, even if no one were prepared to put it into practice.

Admittedly, the world of values is not directly accessible to the majority of us; but there are superior individuals (artists, moral reformers, etc.), whose mission is to discover new values that will eventually circulate as the heritage of common consciousness. The aim of culture is to awaken the largest possible consciousness of values; it

---

6. N. Hartmann, *Ética*, cap. XVI, § *d*.

is not, as is mistakenly supposed, the simple accumulation of knowledge. Culture and the consciousness of values are expressions that signify the same thing. Today's most eminent thinkers share these ideas, which are almost commonplace in axiology (the philosophy of values). This thought is expressed perfectly clearly in the following lines of M. G. Morente:

> *Values, like the world of truth, constitute a realm in which discoveries are possible.* By this I mean that they constitute an ideal kingdom [*un reino irreal*] that does not immediately or completely present itself to our judging perception. There are moral geniuses who have discovered new values that were previously unknown. And after them, those values are perceived by everyone else. Just as electricity was discovered by a few physicists and is familiar to everyone today, charity (in the sense of love) was discovered by Jesus, and has since become a shared value in our common judgment.[7]

Duty: Bridge between the Real and the Ideal

Whoever perceives a pure value, that is, one that has not yet been fulfilled, feels not only the quality of its being valuable, but also the *urgency* of its being fulfilled. If something has value, it *ought to be*. This proposition is self-evident to any consciousness that values. Values, then, are not inert like Plato's Ideas; a dynamic principle pushes them beyond the ideal plane in which they are found and to the plane of real facts. Such dynamism is expressed in consciousness by a sense of duty. Duty in values is like a bridge drawn between being and non-being. It constitutes a characteristic dimension of value: the inclination toward reality.

The world of value reveals itself only to human consciousness, which is why Kant says that "man is a citizen of two worlds," one real, the other ideal. The former imposes itself upon human beings by

---

7. [Manuel G. Morente, *Ensayos sobre el progreso*, prólogo de Juan Miguel Palacios (Madrid: Ediciones Encuentro, 1932), 54. The reference does not appear in the original.]

natural necessity; someone is drawn to the other because of its value. The real world is stronger but lesser; the ideal world is weaker but more valuable. What can we do in the face of this dilemma? According to a traditional way of thinking, each world is completely separate from the other and the roads leading to each diverge. One's only option is to choose one of the two roads. Plato's idealism contains a moral conception of life that teaches us to flee from the sensory world, to elevate ourselves by means of reason to the intelligible world. Descartes, in the modern age, raised an insurmountable barrier between matter and spirit, and even Kant's philosophy establishes a sharp opposition between the world of nature and the world of duty, which represents, at the same time, the kingdom of necessity and the kingdom of freedom.

The drive to be realized in values is enough to understand how communication between the two worlds is possible. The world of value and the world of reality are complementary spheres. The human being is the mediator between these two worlds. We can propose values as the ends of our actions and achieve them in life. Nature is an order that is causally determined, one that moves like a machine, without meaning or purpose. Humans can insert a valuable purpose into that movement and give the world the meaning it lacks. Here we are describing a real process of human effort in history, not a hypothetical act. What we call civilization and culture are precisely the transformation of nature that orients it toward the realization of human ends. The forces of nature are blind in their original state, but humans have dominated and steered them to make them serve a useful purpose. Together, civilization and culture represent an undertaking that tends to elevate nature to a plane in which it acquires meaning and value.

Values can intervene in the march of real events only in the form of purpose. But a teleological order is possible only under the condition of being driven by a mechanical process. To express it in clear terms, one might say that a mechanical process has power but no direction, whereas a finalistic process has direction but not the power to be realized. We can now say that when pulled apart, mechanism and finalism are incomplete orders, but that together, they complement each other. Hartmann says, "The intervention of an entity that pursues ends in the world in which it exists is possible only in a world that is causally determined."[8] Human beings unite everything needed to transform the world into a superior order oriented toward valuable ends. The human being is without question conscious of value and has free will, is capable of setting future goals, and of choosing values as the ends of their action in the world.

---

8. [This is likely a reference to Nicolai Hartmann, *Der Aufbau der realen Welt. Grundriss der allgemeinen Kategorienlehre* [The Structure of the Real World: Outline of a General Theory of Categories] (Berlin: De Gruyter, 1940).]

CHAPTER SIX
Moral Values

Morality is a vast world of which the kingdom of duty is only the top layer. The majority of us are familiar only with this superficial layer and have no idea of the immense volume occupied by the moral sphere. Kant was the first to define morality as a command, which is, in effect, how consciousness requires us to act ethically. We might ignore this command, but only on pain of incurring blame. The philosophical question raised by this phenomenon consists of grounding the validity of the command. Where does the authority of duty come from, the "categorical imperative," as Kant calls it? Kant considers duty a law dictated by reason, which is the ultimate authority of moral validity. The origin of the ethical law is rooted in the subject, and even if the law moves to a transcendental plane, the subject is the creator. If for Kant the subject is the legislator of nature, they are *a fortiori* the legislator of the moral world. That the subject occupies the central position in the world of knowledge and of action is what Kant called his "Copernican Revolution."

One of the characteristic sentiments of the contemporary spirit is that of not wanting to be a legislator of the universe. This was a romantic delusion of the person given to megalomania. The human being of today has ripped off their subjective shell and looks around once again, searching the external world for the norms of their thought and action. The theory of values provides ethical norms with a new foundation that liberates us from Kantian subjectivism. The notion of duty achieves its full significance only once it is connected to the concept of value. The sense of values is the primordial fact of moral consciousness, which then provokes our will to act in accordance with the sense of value. This provocation is what we call duty. Duty is a dimension of value insofar as it summons the will to achieve a value. Kant considered morality rational and stamped duty with the seal of logic. For us, morality is an emotional fact in which duty makes sense only in reference to an end that is deemed valuable.

It is clear that the foundation of an authentic morality must be true consciousness of values. Otherwise, we would encounter forms of conduct that appear to be moral on the surface but that, deep down, give in to prejudice, collective impulses, social mimetism, etc. In real life, the ethical activity of human beings can be reduced to the practice of certain duties whose validity has been imposed on them by tradition. We are referring to practical morality in all its historical forms, as it is lived and accepted by everyone regardless of their social circle. Everyone admits that the person whose conduct effectively conforms to ethical precepts is moral, even if they do not question the foundations of the norms they adopt. But this turns morality into something petty, a mere veneer of action, a purely external formality. We can judge true morality only by knowing the interior of each person, so that we might find out to what extent they are aware of the ends of their action.

There is the kind of person who abandons themselves to a life without purpose, unconscious of their ends, allowing themselves to be carried away by the current and following, at every moment, the path of least resistance. But there are others who approach life with a different attitude. They refuse to give in to external pressure and decide to take responsibility for their lives. For them, living does not amount to mechanically following whatever paths are already mapped out. While searching for a higher purpose in life, they discover a multiplicity of ends that are valuable for different reasons, ends that provoke the will, but which cannot all be pursued at the same time given the limited power of being human. That is why it is necessary to make a choice. The first choice one is forced to make is between giving in to one's natural impulses or repressing them in response to the call of pure value. The challenge is that of deciding which end is superior and thus preferable; and so one suffers from *l'embarras du choix* [an abundance of choice]. Not fully conscious of the multiplicity of life's ends, one cannot make a choice, and whoever does not choose does not, strictly speaking, assume a moral attitude. A condition of assuming a moral attitude is a proper concept of life, which consists in knowing every end and the degree of value that corresponds to each. Here we are not taking into consideration those conceptions [of morality] that, grounded in subjective judgment, are one-sided and reveal a narrowness of vision that is simply the consequence of inexperience or a lack of culture.

Culture is precisely one of the ways humans broaden their horizon until they arrive at a universal vision of things, which gives rise to one's concept of life. We find, then, that there is an internal relation between morality and culture. One cannot be moral, in the noble sense of the word, unless one is cultured. However, so that this idea is not misunderstood, let us be clear that the essence of culture is a correct account of values, not pure knowledge, so that if one does not acquire the right account of values, they do not deserve to be called cultured, however much wisdom they accumulate.[1]

In a broad view of life, which encompasses all human ends, nothing can be considered bad or devoid of value. Every end, however insignificant it may be, has positive value. Moral conflicts that show up in the most common situations of life do not consist in the choice between good and evil, as traditional ethics claims, but in the concurrence of goals that have a different degree of value.[2] The pursuit of something purely hedonistic is not bad in itself; it is bad if it requires

---

1. [Ramos writes, "To believe that we can develop in Mexico an original culture unrelated to the rest of the world constitutes a total misunderstanding of what culture is. The commonest notion is that culture is *pure* knowledge. One fails to recognize the truth that it is rather a function of the spirit destined to humanize reality" (*Profile*, 106).]

2. [In *Making of the Mexican Mind: A Study in Recent Mexican Thought*, Patrick Romanell refers to the distinction between a contest between good and evil and a contest between goods as the distinction between the epic and the tragic sense of life. "The substance of the tragic is not, as the traditional theory of tragedy maintains, the conflict between good and evil. Such is, in fact, the polarity of the epic situation. For the epic hero looks upon the very obstacles he encounters in his ventures as *evil* to be overcome. The stuff that all strictly tragic situations are made of is, rather, the subtler *conflict between goods*, as the greatest tragedies of the world make manifest." *Making of the Mexican Mind* (Notre Dame: University of Notre Dame Press, 1967 [1952]), 22. See also Miguel de Unamuno's *The Tragic Sense of Life*.]

sacrificing a higher purpose. What is bad is to defy higher values for the sake of an inferior end. When there is conflict, then, morality is the act of renouncing what is lower to achieve what is higher.[3]

Every view of life puts one value above the rest, and systematically ties the other values together, so that a lower value is at the same time a means to another end, which leads to another still higher. It is believed that there is a final end that represents the Good par excellence, a good that, sufficient unto itself, renders senseless the pursuit of anything beyond it. The supreme end is the moral value, which serves as the North Star that orients the general axis of existence.

In the typical case, the will does not have that remote end in sight, but is directed toward immediate objects that help it to obtain other objects. Accordingly, the will of habit is utilitarian, given that to serve as the means for something else is the essence of *utility*. So long as the will moves within the region of the useful, it passes from one act to the next, tying life together as a series of commitments. Only when the will desires something for the sake of its value, without any ulterior motive whatsoever, is the will moral. Ethical value is found among those ends that appear to consciousness as the definite conclusion of action.

It is undeniable that the will can aim directly at a moral value. Kant's opinion is that an act is good only if it is done "out of duty." One's conduct is praiseworthy only if their basic intention is good. But is this true? Isn't someone who does good with the sole aim of being good thinking only of oneself? Doesn't this attitude merely conceal the soul of the Pharisee, a disguised egoism? Surely, the best intention is not the one that points directly at moral value. A truthful person does not work at being truthful, but to make the truth known. If the knowledge of truth were not valuable, would truthfulness be morally good? It can be argued that moral value is the result of achieving non-moral values. One thing is the value brought to fruition; the other, the value of fulfillment. The intention does not

---

3. E. Spranger, *Formas de vida*, pp. 299 *ss.*

face moral value, which appears, as Scheler says, "behind the act."[4] The theory just expounded here greatly expands the field of moral life, since one can infer from it that ethical significance is implied in the fulfillment of any value.

Values that are specifically moral are distinguished from other values in that they are embodied only in the human being. It does not make sense to judge the morality of a triangle, a house, or a tree. Moral values are never values of things, but exclusively of persons. It is precisely by virtue of one's moral quality that someone falls under the category of a *person*. Someone is considered a person insofar as they are an end in themselves and cannot be used as a means.[5] If the concept of a final end is not vacuous and if ethics attributes concrete substance to it, the supreme moral value, that end must be the individual human being. "The human being is not made for morality; morality is made for the human being." It is inconceivable that morality leads to a result beyond human interest. Even religious morality is of the same opinion. If for Christianity virtue leads to the "kingdom of God," it is because it is found, according to the words of the Gospel, in the interior of the human being. Here, ethics confronts the most pressing question put to knowledge: What is the vocation of being human?[6] Fichte responds to this question this way:

> As surely as man is a rational being, he is the end of his own existence; i.e. he does not exist to the end that something else may be, but he exists absolutely because he himself is to be—his being is its own

---

4. ["Auf den Rücken" in the German original. See Max Scheler, *Formalism in Ethics and Non-Formal Ethics of Values*, trans. Manfred S. Frings and Roger L. Funk (Evanston, IL: Northwestern University Press, 1973); and *The Nature of Sympathy*, trans. Peter Heath Hamden (London: Routledge and Kegan Press, 1954). *Wesen und Formen der Sympathie* was translated into Spanish by José Gaos in 1923.]

5. Kant, *Fundamentación de la metafísica de las costumbres* (trad. De M. G. Morente), pp. 77 ss.

6. [Ramos uses the term *destino*, here translated as "vocation," following the Spanish translation of Fichte. Fichte uses the term *Bestimmung*, which can mean determination, assignment, or purpose. See Johann Gottlieb Fichte, *Einige Vorlesungen über die Bestimmung des Gelehrten* (1794).]

ultimate object—or, what is the same thing, man cannot, without contradiction to himself, demand an object of his existence. He is, because he is. This character of absolute being—of existence for his own sake alone—is his characteristic or vocation, in so far as he is considered solely as a rational being.[7]

But since humans do not live alone, one can only achieve their vocation in a community. Moral values have a social dimension in that they appear only in acts whose intention refers to others or to society as a whole. If in considering motives and ends I dispense with my individuality in order to see things from a wider human perspective, if I judge *sub specie humanitatis*, of what importance is my personal desire vis-à-vis human values? August Messer says, "In this way we arrive at the values we think of, first, when we talk about morality, and which seem to form a special group alongside spiritual values, which are of a different nature. If we look at them more closely, they are values that are realized in our attitude toward our fellow human beings, either isolated or as part of a community, and they are therefore social and altruistic values."[8]

---

7. J. G. Fichte, *El Destino del hombre* (trad. De E. Ovejero y Maury), p. 234. [Johann Gottlieb Fichte, "The Vocation of the Scholar," in *Works*, trans. William Smith (The Perfect Library), 2013.]

8. [This quote is likely a reference to August Messer, *La estimativa o la filosofía de los valores en la actualidad*, translated by Pedro Caravia, Madrid, 1932. August Messer was often translated into Spanish in the 1920s and 1930s. His *Philosophische Grundlegung der Pädagogik* [Philosophical Foundation of Pedagogy] was translated in 1927 by José Rovira; *Weltanschauung und Erziehung* [Worldview and Education] was published in 1929 and translated by Joaquín Xirau; *Geschichte der Philosophie im 19. Jahrhundert* appeared in 1932, translated by José Gaos; *Einführung in die Psychologie und die psychologischen Richtungen der Gegenwart* was translated in 1934 by Julia Rodríguez Danilewski.]

CHAPTER SEVEN

The Human Being as Freedom

Philosophical arguments in defense of freedom did not fare well in modern thought until the end of the nineteenth century. This was especially true of philosophical schools directly influenced by natural science. Mechanism [*mecanicismo*],[1] materialism, and positivism emphatically deny freedom; they consider it incompatible with the idea of universal causality. As the scientific conception of the cosmos became more unified, the traditional notion of freedom had less chance of surviving. Its collapse brought about the reassessment of every judgment about human beings who, deprived of their freedom, lost one of their highest values and were lowered to the rank of slaves of nature.

One achievement of contemporary philosophy has been to demonstrate that the negation of freedom emerged because of a mistaken point of view that judged freedom from afar. Freedom is originally a human phenomenon that should not be discussed using analogies borrowed from the physical world, or interpreted using principles that discount its inherent character. All that was needed to quickly change perspectives on a solution was to move the problem to the realm of human ontology. Bergson was one of the first philosophers to see the confusion of points of view that assess freedom, and only by reframing the problem has he shown that a full philosophical justification of freedom is possible.[2] Freedom should be considered an ontological trait of being human, and thus, it is a

---

1. [Here the word is *mecanicismo* rather than *maquinismo*. Ramos is referring specifically to mechanical explanations of biological phenomenon. See chapter 1, fn. 5.]

2. [This is the main thesis of Bergson's *Essai sur les données immédiates de la conscience* [Time and Free Will: An Essay on the Immediate Data of Consciousness] (1889) and *Matière et Memoire* [Matter and Memory] (1896).]

question to be investigated by anthropology. Hartmann developed one of the most plausible if little-known theories of freedom in his great work of ethics.[3] I believe it might be of interest to discuss some of his most significant conclusions in order to present the reader with a brief introduction to this important theory, which is the final word in philosophy on the problem of human freedom.[4]

Hartmann has put forward an original theory of freedom, worth reproducing here, even if only schematically, in order to clarify many things that are left vague in modern theories of freedom. He does not present his theory in order to resolve all the problems concerning freedom once and for all. Carefully and cautiously, he meditates on every aspect of the issue, appreciating its difficulty, and he refrains from exceeding the limits of human knowledge. His plan is to outline a theory of freedom that satisfies certain scientific requirements, and to do so with the least amount of metaphysics possible. Moral freedom is a fact that, so to speak, straddles the line between the rational and irrational, in such a way that it is only partially the object of our knowledge.

The most serious theoretical difficulty in justifying freedom is to explain how it is possible in a world universally governed by causal determination. Before Kant, philosophers believed that freedom and determinism were two terms irreducibly opposed. Kant was the first to destroy this assumption, reframing the problem anew to demonstrate that freedom and causality are not mutually exclusive. Kant's discovery set the problem on a new course in the history of

---

3. [See Nicolai Hartmann, *Ethics*, 3 vols., trans. Stanton Coit (London: George Allen & Unwin, 1932).]

4. [Hartmann was highly regarded when Ramos was writing this text and is not written about much today. José Gaos said Hartmann's *Ontology* was "the most important philosophical work since Christian Wolf's in the 18th Century." Letter to Salvador Azuela, August 29, 1955, in Gaos, *Complete Works*, vol. 19 (Mexico: UNAM, 1999), 347. Gaos spent ten years translating the three volumes into Spanish, although by the time he finished he believed Hartmann's work was "ciencia que nace muerta" [a still-born science]. Letter to Vera Yamuni, January 21, 1963, in José Gaos's Archive, Instituto de Investigaciones Filosóficas, UNAM, folder 9, file 64845. The rest of this chapter was previously published in *Revista de Estudios Universtarios* 1, no. 2 (October–December 1939).]

philosophy, although he was far from solving it definitively. If one strips Kant's thesis of its metaphysics, it can be reduced to the following proposition: human beings are subject to two independent kinds of determination, the natural law and the moral law. This idea in no way violates the principle of causality, but it does establish that there are two different types of causal determination. Determinism is not the problem in justifying freedom, according to Hartmann; deterministic monism is. One cannot obtain more specific details concerning the nature of freedom from Kant's theory other than that its determining factor is the "moral law," which derives from "practical reason." Hartmann reproaches Kant for locating the principle of freedom in a supra-individual consciousness, which amounts to removing it from the subject itself.

In the current state of philosophical knowledge, we know that the moral law is a determination of values *sui generis*, one that assumes the form of finality when it manifests itself in action. Only humans can insert teleological activity into the world, because they are the only being endowed with a consciousness that senses value and that is capable of proposing it as an end of their actions. Humans, then, are faced with two causal series into which they can introduce their conduct: mechanical determination and axiological determination. Therefore, the human being is the only factor that can mediate between the world of values and the real world. The finalist nexus is transformed the moment it is realized in causality, because the means are the cause and the end is the effect. That is why Hartmann concludes that finality is not possible except in a world that is causally determined. The essence of the mechanical process requires nothing other than the causal sequence, which is indifferent to any orientation toward an end. In this way, in virtue of its indifference [toward ends] a causal series admits at any point in its temporal development an outside determination that gives it meaning. Its transformation into a teleological process does not annul its purely mechanistic essence at all. This is what civilization does when it takes advantage of natural forces, which are originally blind: it imposes on them an end useful to us. Thus, the supposed radical antagonism between mechanical causality and finalism does not exist. On the contrary, they are two processes that mutually complement each other, causality receiving from the other the meaning it lacks, and the teleological process taking from the first the power it lacks to realize itself. Between these two processes there is a relation of condition and conditioned. In a way, the teleological process depends on the causal, which is stronger but lower. In exchange, the finalist process is weaker but higher in rank and is free to orient its movement in any direction.

The sphere of values constitutes an ideal domain independent of the real world. But its autonomy should not be confused with human moral freedom. Axiological determination does not drive this freedom. More often than not, philosophers believe that moral freedom is possible only in a world that moves teleologically. But the most superficial rethinking notices that this is impossible. If for a moment we grant that the world is universally governed by teleological law, such that it unfolds as a prearranged plan both in detail and as a whole, then all of our acts would be predestined, and freedom would be utterly impossible in a universe governed by inexorable mechanical laws. If values entailed a necessary obligation, the human (in relation to values) would be an automaton that fulfilled, perfectly, its mission to realize them. But this kind of determination is only an ideal demand, which the will can ignore. In principle, it is possible for us to rebel against duties that values impose upon us. The human, then, is an imperfect mediator. But this imperfection is a virtue because if we were not free vis-à-vis the demands of values, we would not be moral entities. Humans, then, are free in a double sense: both in respect to the natural law and in respect to axiological determination.

Freedom should not be sought in that which transcends the individual, but in their interiority, as something that belongs to them, so that, strictly speaking, their will is inherently free. Now, if upon reflection, freedom appears as the capacity to disobey an imperative given by values or to avoid natural impulses, it should not thereby be identified as "indeterminism." That would amount to conceiving of its essence as something negative, in the Scholastic sense of *liberum arbitrarium indiferentiae* [undetermined free will]. Freedom is either a positive force, a decision of the will whose origin is self-determination, or it is an empty concept that, depriving freedom of any substance, makes it unintelligible. Freedom is not a violation of the principle of causality. What is needed to explain it, as Hartmann says, is an *extra burst* of determination that the will introduces into causal networks. Such freedom in a "positive sense" is possible if the causal nexus is constituted in the world by different types of determination, each of which enjoys a certain autonomy.

In this sense, freedom is not an exceptional phenomenon found only in the human being; it is common among beings that are tiered on different layers of existence. Compared to inanimate nature, the animal is free, as is evidenced by its movement and sensibility. Compared to organic life, to which it is attached, consciousness is free. And so on. When the problem of moral freedom is viewed from a wider perspective, the dualism associated with determinism dissolves into pluralism. Each layer of being seems to be endowed with a characteristic type of determination. Within the ideal sphere of being, we of course find logical necessity, which, in the words of Leibniz, for example, is expressed in "the principle of sufficient reason." Next comes mathematical necessity, which governs all calculation according to its own peculiar laws of deduction. In the field of physical reality, there is a layered series of independent forms of determination: mechanical determination, biological determination, psychological determination. Finally, the spirit emerges as the highest layer, whose processes are also bound by their own laws.

The freedom that corresponds to each of these layers is not absolute; each one is conditioned by the previous, such that there is no personality without consciousness, no consciousness without organic life, no organic life without a natural mechanical structure, no mechanism without mathematical order. But in each order there appears to be an element that cannot be reduced to the previous, which constitutes precisely what is new about each one. If an organism lives as a corporeal being, tied to the physical-chemical order, the same life in it that manifests itself as nutrition, growth, and reproduction is a phenomenon that can be explained only by specifically biological principles. Biological determination is relatively free in respect to mechanical determination. Hartmann does not grant the "contingency of natural laws," as did Boutroux, who believed that this was the only way to explain freedom.[5] That would be to make the mistake of identifying freedom with indeterminism and give it a negative meaning. Within each layer, the law particular to it is fulfilled necessarily in every case. Freedom is understood as a new form of determination that each being introduces into the inferior structure that sustains it. It is, then, freedom in a positive sense.

If the previous arguments are not definitive proof of freedom, they are still of great value, in theory, because they demonstrate that the affirmation of free will does not contradict the idea that the world is uniformly ordered by the principle of causality. If these arguments are not sufficient to prove its actuality, they are at least enough to fully justify its possibility. But neither does that mean that there is no factual proof of freedom. Hartmann rightly maintains that such proof is found in certain phenomena of moral life, such as *responsibility*, *accountability*, and *guilt*. Admittedly, none of these phenomena has absolute evidentiary value because there is no absolute proof; however, they come closest to this ideal of demonstration. With regard to the consciousness of freedom as an argument in favor of the freedom of consciousness, to use Hartmann's expression, opponents of freedom from Spinoza on have rejected it, claiming that it is simply an illusion. This does not thereby strengthen the determinist's position, since they are obligated to explain what gave birth to this illusion and what the grounds of its origins are, and they have not done so. In any case, the argument based on the consciousness of freedom is subject to objections. In response, Hartmann notes that responsibility, accountability, and guilt are indubitable facts of moral life that even the harshest (impartial) critic cannot interpret as mere illusions. Generally, an illusion is born in the consciousness of a strong, vital desire to protect the subject. Even in the most unfavorable cases where responsibility and guilt work against personal interest, both impose themselves on consciousness, and the subject has no choice but to accept them. If one grants that the existence of responsibility, accountability, and guilt is

---

5. [Besides his *Ethics*, see Nicolai Hartmann, *Possibility and Actuality*, trans. Stephanie Adair and Alex Scott (Berlin: De Gruyter, 2013 [1938]). Boutroux's most influential text on this topic is *The Contingency of the Laws of Nature*, trans. Fred Rothwell (Chicago and London: Open Court Publishing Company, 1916).]

indisputable, one is also forced to grant the existence of freedom. It is so obvious that such phenomena imply the existence of freedom, in a real sense, that any explanation is self-evident.

Hartmann's most original idea affirms, in opposition to a traditional prejudice, that the existence of freedom is not only compatible with causal determination but also requires it. And when he lays out this theory, he presents the whole sphere of moral activity under a new aspect, which makes visible its connection to inferior forms of life. If the universe is thought to be governed by determinism, the human being appears to be downgraded to the rank of a purely biological entity. Likewise, a universal finalism elevates nature above humans and denies that they are ethical beings. Both theories, then, share a common denominator. The sense of a new relationship, which Hartmann establishes between free moral activity and other forms of determination, is clarified by certain laws of dependence which he formulates in the following way: (1) *The law of strength*. The highest types of determination depend on the lowest, but the inverse is not true. So, the highest is the most conditioned, the most dependent, and in this sense the weakest. The lowest is the most unconditioned, the most elemental, and in this sense the strongest. (2) *The law of matter*. Each inferior type is considered raw material for that which is above it. (3) *The law of freedom*. Each type higher than the inferior is a new structure that is raised above it. It has a boundless end above the lower form of determination. And regardless of its dependence on it, the higher type is free.[6]

It seems to me that these principles have the merit of destroying a prejudice that the facts prove wrong each step of the way: that the highest forms of human life are stronger than the inferior, even though everyday experience teaches us that the most noble values buckle under the weight of petty interests. At the same time, Hartmann's laws challenge another assumption just as false and vulgar as the previous one. It consists of estimating a value in proportion to its strength, in thinking that what is stronger is more valuable.

---

6. [Among the laws of dependence there is a fourth term that Ramos doesn't mention: *indifference* (the other three being *strength*, *matter*, and *freedom*).]

With this principle, the table of values is completely reversed, and it falls into the absurdity of considering the values of nature superior to authentically human values. Hartmann invites us to separate strength from value completely, recognizing that even though natural processes are superior in strength, they remain inferior to spiritual processes from the point of view of pure value. In his theories about anthropology, Scheler maintains a similar idea; but he takes it to the extreme of claiming that the spirit is essentially impotent.[7]

The merit of Hartmann's thesis is not just in what it separates, but in what it unites. Hartmann helps us to see that if the more valuable forms of determination are weaker, they can take advantage of the inferior values in order to fulfill their ends. If we apply this idea to the problems of culture today, the goal of turning mechanical civilization—when guided by wisdom—into an instrument of freedom for the sake of spiritual development is justified.

One important question still remains unresolved: What is the nature of the determining principle of freedom? Here we reach the limit of rationality concerning the problem. It is one of those final questions that human understanding is unable to answer. And the problem of freedom is not the only unanswerable question. On the same footing are questions like these: What is reality? What is being? What is the ideal? etc. The most accurate data Hartmann is able to offer as a response to this line of questioning are limited to defining freedom "as the autonomy of the person as opposed to the autonomy of values."[8] To understand this definition, recall that the determining principle of the will is not the duty that originates in values, since that duty can sometimes be violated, demonstrating that such an imperative lacks effective power. Thus, it is necessary that the will make an imperative its own and puts it to work, lending its own strength. In the act of freedom, there is, in a certain sense, a collaboration of the will and values. But the determining principle is a positive force rooted in the person. About this there can be no doubt.

---

7. [See Scheler, *The Human Place in the Cosmos*, 47.]

8. [Hartmann, *Ethics*, vol. 3: Moral Freedom, 16e–17c.]

Chapter Seven: The Human Being as Freedom

Hartmann makes this case in the most convincing way. There are conflicts of value that are not resolved in the table of values and that, for the valuing consciousness, constitute genuine antinomies. But in real life such antinomies must be resolved and we are obligated to work them out. This is where the initiative of the individual comes into play: faced with a conflict, we must choose by an act of the sovereign will, taking responsibility for the results of his deeds. Only a being capable of true initiative, that is, only a being that is *free*, can do that. And, in being exercised, that initiative involves a real power. *How* the power of freedom is acted upon is not a problem for thought. Hartmann says that freedom is a finalist determination. The claim that there exists freedom of the will does not mean that it can always be found in every moment of life. Hartmann recognizes that one is not responsible for many of the acts they commit. Freedom, he says, is a summit of humanity, and it is not always easy for individuals to maintain that height.

CHAPTER EIGHT
Person and Personality

The person is a general phenomenon in which human spirituality is projected, and personality is the highest degree reached only by a few individuals. The value of personality was discovered in the Renaissance and the idea that it represents the highest goal of humanization has since remained part of our culture. No fact appears to be more self-evident than personality, since, even without an antecedent notion of it, we can discern its existence in those who possess it. But when we try to isolate it in thought, a clear profile of it evaporates, and its distinctive traits resist being captured in clear formulae. This topic raises a number of problems that fall under the purview of philosophical anthropology, since it concerns a fact that pertains exclusively to the human being. The category of person is applied only to the human being, at the exclusion of all other living beings.

Language seems to differentiate between person and personality. In principle, we grant that everyone is a person, but we reserve personality for a smaller number. While *person* is a descriptor that ranges over the entire human species, the term *personality* is applied to a smaller field.

We call someone a *person*, not because they are a physical or psychic entity, but a moral one. When one freely acts, thinks, or feels, *person* is the physiognomy the subject gives to oneself through the spontaneous exercise of one's most intimate will. This physiognomy can be distinguished from the profile that emerges from each individual's character. The individual acquires their character at birth; however, one gives a personality to oneself, superimposing it over one's psychic-physical character like an ideal mask. The etymology of this word can give us a glimmer of its meaning. [Ludwig] Klages writes:

> "Person" is the Latin "persona," which is derived from "personare" = "to sound through," and originally denotes the mask through which the ancient actor speaks, then the part he has to play, and finally "character"

or "personality." Thus the Latin name for the tragic mask has taken root as standing designation for the essence of man; the mask which begins to live only when the actor's voice sounds through it. We do not ask here how far this peculiar duality affords a useful hint even to the metaphysics of the duplicity in question, and are content to record that the original etymology in fact uses "person" to denote something twofold: a face which is lifeless in itself, and a voice which sounds through it, which in original drama is the voice of a god.[1]

In effect, personality is like a role we play and it appears only in social relations, in its public performance. However, unlike the theater actor, this role is of our own creation; we are, at the same time, author and actor. If personality has a social dimension, it is distinguished from purely social acts that are expressed in preestablished forms and which we assume as they are presented to us, already made. When we follow a custom or fulfill a social function, we abdicate individual will and subordinate it to a certain generic prescription. Personality appears as a form of human life in which two dimensions join together: the individual and the social.

Without question, personality is rooted and based in the psycho-physical character of the individual, but it is something distinct from mere individuality. Personality installs itself on top of individuality as a complement that is tasked with instructing and guiding it, that is, as a force that governs it. Individuality and personality are two distinct layers of the human being arranged hierarchically so that personality is higher in rank. Personality, then, is not a phenomenon determined by laws immanent in the individual; it is not a biological or psychological fact, but a phenomenon of a spiritual order.

Personality awakens the idea of lordship and control an individual has over the actions of their life; it belongs to whoever does not allow oneself to be dragged along by their inclinations or by their surrounding circumstances, but who pulls oneself together and gives their activity direction and its own signature. The kind of person who,

---

1. [Ludwig Klages, *The Science of Character*, trans. W. H. Johnston (London: George Allen & Unwin, 1929), 41–42.]

beyond subjective motives, always obeys the norms of truth, morality, and aesthetics, and who, in so doing, betrays that a superior will is in control. They allow their most inward voice to resonate through the will, revealing their highest values. At the center of one's personality is the true self. Only the decisions that originate from this center are characterized as spontaneous and active, as opposed to all passive movement. This center is the supreme authority that approves or disapproves of every kind of urge that arises in any given part of a human being.

If personality originates in the individual self, its direction, however, is essentially centrifugal. There are impulses that are directed exclusively at the affirmation of individuality; these are centripetal movements. For personality, the individual is only a means of affirming supra-individual values. Of course, personality belongs only to the individual and cannot be transmitted or reproduced; everyone has to create their own personality. But the realization of personality without the consciousness of individuality is possible, as proven by the case of the Greeks. The consciousness of individuality is a discovery of the modern period, which, at times, tries to make use of personality in order to affirm itself. It is one of the many resources that so-called individualism employs to establish itself, but at bottom individuality is something very distinct from aspiring to personality. The roots of personality are not to be found in the *being-for-itself* of the subject, but in its *being-for-the-other*. One condition of achieving personality is not to think about it or make personality the deliberate aim of life. When it is proposed as an end that is pursued consciously, it is almost certain that such an attitude is concealing individualistic ambition. In this case, the internal contradiction rules out realizing the personality desired. This false attitude often strays toward the futile imitation of a foreign personality that is taken as a model.

Personality manifests as something coherent, a unity across an individual's behavior. It appears as a stable meaning that guides the most heterogeneous activities of existence. This does not mean that in order to appreciate a specific personality one has to account for the entire history of an individual's development. The subject does not inject their personality into every act, but one act alone might suffice to reveal the whole of it. Personal acts are those that the individual achieves through the intervention of their whole being. In them personality shows itself as the unique standard stamped on the concrete work—an unmistakable seal. The sign of singular unity is essential to the life of a person, as it has already been shown to be a distinctive feature in isolated psychological phenomena (Dilthey, [William] Stern).[2] There is also a functional connection among the different parts of psychological life that, in proportion, convert certain structural configurations into "psychologic types" (the intellectual, the intuitive type, the sensitive type, etc.). On top of this structural base, modifications can settle in, determined by the *ethos*, which consists of the particular position that each individual takes with respect to values. *Ethos* is a system of valuative selection. In the taste of every individual, in their sympathies and repugnancies, the same manner of preferring or rejecting is constantly at play. Such dispositions toward valuing things influence one's psychological physiognomy, giving it a determinate structure depending on the class of values one prefers. The nuances of personality are revealed, above all, in the things the individual chooses and leaves out to form a world of one's own.

Without a doubt, psychic character and personality interact. Character is the raw material of personality and also the framework that delimits its possibilities. Within a psycho-physical type there is only room for a determinate kind of personality. But this kind of personality is the power that governs the forces of character and channels them toward certain objective values. The discovery of values affects the configuration of psychological life. Values are like new points of interest capable of awaking or pooling together feelings, images, and ideas that alter the panorama of interior life. Thus, in this way, when

---

2. [See, for example, William Stern, *Person und Sache: System der philosophischen Weltanschauung. Erster Band: Ableitung und Grundlehre* [Person and Thing: System of a Philosophical Worldview, vol. 1, Rational and Basic Tenets] (Leipzig: Barth, 1906): "A person is an entity that, though consisting of many parts, forms an inherently valuable unity and, as such, constitutes, over and above its functioning parts, a unitary, self-activated, goal-oriented being," quoted in James T. Lamiell, *William Stern (1871–1938): A Brief Introduction to His Life and Works* (Lengerich: Papst Science Publishers, 2010), 97.]

values circulate around a subject, they transform one's private life and their interiority becomes a person. Hartmann says that one is a person only insofar as they are an axiological entity, a being endowed with a valuative consciousness, as well as a "bearer of values." If one were a pure subject, one would be an entity driven by natural impulses alone, without any notion of values; however, even though we can conceive of such an entity, we can't be sure that one exists anywhere. As a person, aside from being a subject, the human is a being that is conscious of values and that is a value in itself. *Person* is a new category, higher in rank than the category of *subject*. What is the relation between the subject and the person? Can personality be attributed to something that does not have the character of a subject? Certain metaphysical implications concerning the concept of personality depend on the answer to this question. If, as Scheler thinks, being a psychophysical subject is not required for attributing personhood, we will have to grant personality to purely abstract entities, such as society, the nation, the universe, etc. But since a person requires a will in order to realize oneself, a conscious action that cannot be conceived of outside of concrete subjects, it is clear that their reality is impossible without the existence of a subjective base. This question will now be treated in greater detail below.

The Metaphysics of Personality

Personality is an ontological category of human existence, which is difficult to capture within customary forms of thought alone. It cannot be thought of as part of the idea of a substance lodged in the deepest recesses of the human being, nor as a pure abstract essence that hovers above the individual mind and serves as a model of behavior. The entity of the person manifests its real existence in action, and not just in one particular species of action, such as practical conduct, be it moral, political, or economic. Intellectual, artistic, religious life, etc., is also action. In every occupation, one can reveal a personality. There are personal ways of thinking, feeling, imagining, believing, loving, etc. [Eduard] Spranger tried to classify and define different types of personality, which he considered a "structure of sense" that originates in the intuition of a value.³

Personality is not, as might be supposed, a spiritual structure fixed beforehand, representing, so to speak, an *a priori* form of action. Rather, it is the meaning of an infinite process that moves toward a goal just within reach. We could say that personality shares a programmatic character with life in general.

Max Scheler, to whom we owe the most complete investigation of this topic, identifies spirit and person (analyzed from the point of view of ethics). This is the necessary form of the existence of the spirit. The idea of an impersonal spirit is contradictory to him. The spirit is essentially a pure actuality that has being only as it is being carried out; it is a complex set of acts ordered within a unity. The person is, so to speak, the center of their acts, the common source of them, not their starting point, but something that is born and lives through those acts. Each real and concrete act (for example, the act of thinking or desiring), carries within itself the *totum* and the particular essence of the personality that springs from it.

Now, insofar as the person is completely in the present moment, it cannot be the object of internal perception. Only in its performance is it lived immediately; its only way of presenting itself is the performance itself. It cannot be objectified, not even retroactively. We can only focus on the being of our person and participate in the being of others by carrying out its free acts, in ourselves and by ourselves, identifying ourselves with the intentions behind them.

We should recall that the acts in which personality is realized are those that obey objective norms of value and annul individual motives that may stand opposed to them. In a word, the subject recognizes and abides by the True, the Good, and the Beautiful, as the supreme authorities in life. But, at the same time, personality appears as a value distinct from those that condition it, even when it springs from them. One is the value fulfilled and the other is the value of being performed. The first can be very different in nature and remains

---

3. [See Eduard Spranger, *Types of Men*, trans. P. J. W. Pigors (New York: G. E. Stechert Company, 1928).]

attached to the work of, for example, science, art, etc. The second belongs exclusively to the author of the work; it is the value specific to personality and its nature is always the same. It is a moral value. Now, this "morality" [*eticidad*] of the person, on account of its singularity, is distinguished from the remaining ethical values. But whatever its singularity amounts to, the person is a moral condition. The value intrinsic to being human, that which does not depend on any outside circumstance, is measured by the degree of personality that one is able to achieve. We acquire our moral status when we act of our own volition and live according to our true self. It is true that ethical laws are general, but in truth they are not carried out if they are not previously assimilated by the individual spirit. Strictly speaking, authentic morality is only that which is lived personally.

Personality as Duty

Recognizing the full ethical value of personality necessarily entails that its fulfillment is imposed as a duty. The value of personality was discovered in the Renaissance and was raised to the highest rank among human values. Since its incorporation into modern culture, only naturalist conceptions of the human being and those that consider us merely a social product have overlooked the value of personality. Romanticism has defended it, frequently confusing it with inclination toward individualism.

One has the responsibility of being true to oneself. This imperative has been captured in succinct formulae throughout history. Among the Greeks, Pindar said, "Become who you are." In the moral teachings of Fichte, we encounter the following words: "Fulfill your vocation."[4] Personality as a norm is also in Hartmann's maxim, which inverts one way of formulating the categorical imperative: "Act in such a way that the maxim of your will cannot become a universal rule of conduct."[5]

---

4. [See Johann Gottlieb Fichte, *The Vocation of Man*, trans. Peter Preuss (Indianapolis: Hackett Publishing Company, 1987).]

5. [Hartmann, *Ethics*, vol. 2, 357: "So act, that the maxim of thy will could never become the principle of a universal legislation without a remainder," 134.]

Only prejudice or a one-sided vision of the world leads to the belief in an irreducible antinomy between collective and individual values. In fulfilling the most common duties in life, there is always room for leaving an individual mark. However, there are many who are dominated by an obsession with collective values and insist on deliberately drowning out all personal expression. Nor can it be doubted that in certain cases this attitude is the result of an absence of the subjective conditions to differentiate oneself. We must keep in mind that, given the constitution of human beings, not every individual is fertile ground for spiritual differentiation. In the average person, individuality barely reveals itself in faint brushstrokes. Their conduct is determined by social imitation, shared impulses, etc. Their ethics is completely impersonal and they are governed by the formulae of duty learned through customary morality. Among the undifferentiated crowd, those destined to individuality are in the minority. They do not conform to commonplace morality and their behavior exhibits an eagerness to distinguish oneself. But if this inclination leads one to sacrifice basic values, it is because the individual lacks the moral strength required to form a true personality.

Those capable of becoming great personalities bear a huge historical responsibility. Their resistance to customary values destines them to create new values. Once these values become objectified in the form of cultural products, they become a permanent part of the public domain and are popularized. Then there will be others who, fleeing from the commonplace, will find new values, which will in turn spread widely and so on *ad infinitum*. It is important to keep in mind that the collective values of today were exceptional yesterday and were only understood and loved by a few. The mission of a great personality is to keep the human spirit from coming to a halt. Socially, they are the individuals who incite revolution, who, by virtue of their distaste

---

Hartmann adds, "One might also express it in this way: Never act merely according to a system of universal values but always at the same time in accordance with the individual values of thine own personal nature. Or: Always act not only in accord with thy universal conscience (the sense of moral value in general) but also at the same time follow thy private conscience (thine individual sense of values)."]

for established values, drive culture forward by discovering ever-new horizons for human aspiration.

Collective Personalities

Are there "collective personalities" in the same sense as there are individual personalities? We cannot deny the fact that people work together to achieve goals beyond the reach of individuals. Nations engage in commerce, take on debt, wage war, produce culture, and assume a kind of common responsibility. Here values are not realized by isolated persons, but in virtue of solidarity with other people. Scheler sees solidarity as the basis of "collective persons," who are arranged hierarchically on top of the simple individual person. According to this theory, which is part of his system of ethics, the value of persons depends on their relation to other persons of a progressively higher order, at the summit of which is the person of God. Such complex personalities do not exist in every form of human community. They of course do not exist in "the crowd," a social unity constituted by communication and involuntary imitation that is driven by instinct. Among animals, it is called the herd, a horde; among people, the multitude. The person also does not exist in groups that Scheler calls "vital communities," such as, for example, the family, the tribe, the clan, or a social or professional class. There is even a distinct third kind of collective unity, formed consciously through promises or contracts between individuals, a unity that Scheler names "society" plain and simple. In this category, we should also include purely legal associations, to which Scheler does not attribute personality.[6]

Only collective unities of a higher order are persons in the sense of the word explained above. Such communities are those that have a spiritual life expressed in intellectual, sentient, and emotional activities, etc. Above purely biological existence, the group recognizes a higher order of values and has the will to accomplish them. They are

---

6. [See Max Scheler, *Formalism in Ethics and Non-Formal Ethics of Value*, trans. Manfred S. Frings and Roger L. Funk (Evanston, IL: Northwestern University Press, 1973 [1913–1916]). In 1942, Hilario Rodríguez Sanz translated it as *Ética. Nuevo ensayo de fundamentación de un personalismo ético*.]

highly differentiated communities in which personality flourishes in concrete individuals whose spiritual lives do not isolate them but bring them together in solidarity. Nations and "circles of culture," such as Europe and the Orient, etc., are good examples of collective personalities. Scheler's personalism underscores the fact that the person only makes sense as a form of spiritual solidarity among people and is opposed to all individualistic inclination. To aspire consciously to affirm one's own personality is the surest way to lose it. Personal values are absolutely unrealizable as immediate ends of the will. Both individual and collective persons (nations, for example) can add to their values only by surrendering, even to the point of oblivion or self-abdication, to purely objective and impersonal ends and values. The true treasure of personality only offers itself to one who does not pursue it and it hides from the one who is looking specifically for it. Nationalism does not think about this, since its deliberate intention is to impress upon "the collective soul" a mark of originality by means of culture.

For Scheler, collective personalities have the same metaphysical status as individual personalities because the person is a supra-conscious entity that does not depend on the existence of a body, the psychic self, or a will. But in order to fulfill itself, the person requires a unifying and transcendent activity, directed toward values, which would not be possible without consciousness and a will, which only exist in concrete individuals. Therefore, the person cannot be separated from a real subject, even though it is essentially different from simple subjectivity. It is possible to imagine, even if as a matter of fact we never encounter it, a purely psychological subject, absolutely lacking a personality. But a free-floating personality without a substratum is a fantasy. If we are talking about the personality as something positive, then, it is necessary to attribute it to a real subject. Hartmann says, "Personality exists only on a basis of subjectivity, just as subjectivity exists only on a basis of organic life, and life on a basis of the whole subordinate uniformity of nature. This categorial gradation is not irreversible."[7]

---

7. [Hartmann, *Ethics*, vol. 1, 326.]

One might think that it is possible for a collectivity to function as a real subject placed on top of individuals. For this to be the case, it would be necessary to demonstrate that it is therefore inseparable from an individual subject still impossible to imagine. If a person, in order to exist, requires a unity of subjective consciousness and a will that freely chooses its ends, then there is a "collective will," a "general consciousness," outside of individuals. Clearly, that is the only being that meets those conditions. We cannot deny the existence of a collective consciousness, will, or responsibility, but it would have to exist in individuals because outside of individuals there is no common subject that underwrites them. However, we can observe that the collectivity has a life that is expressed in the characteristics analogous to those of a person, but that is because it is in persons in which the community is represented. In its place, the ruler, legislator, and leader are individuals in charge of interpreting the common will, of anticipating the ends that it must aim toward. Likewise, thinkers, artists, and sages—in a word, all those who endow society with spirit—shape it in their own image. Even granting that the psychological structure of such individuals is conditioned by the society in which they live, they are the only ones who can have personality, which they in turn project onto the whole of society as an enlarged image.

CHAPTER NINE
Conclusion

At the start of this book, I tried to describe and explain an aspect of the contemporary crisis that is the most detrimental to human values. It is a tear in the human fabric brought about by internal contradictions that distort the positive meaning of civilization. This includes a demonic impulse that, having escaped the power of human will, has created destructive forces that turn against the interests of humanity. When we look at the present state of the world, it is easy to view civilization as a monster that, having broken free from its chains, threatens to destroy its own master and creator. That is, civilization, contrary to its original destiny, has become an instrument of death, not life. Thus, we have arrived at the paradoxical situation of having to defend ourselves against our own civilization. This situation has produced within itself negative forces that can destroy freedom, personality, and the spiritual life of the human being. To achieve this end, civilization employs a thousand resources to dull judgment, weaken moral strength, infect the intellect, and conquer the will. It has done so to such a degree that we seem to desire our own destruction, and it has also found a philosophy to justify it by disguising it as a benefit on which to pin our highest aspirations. Fortunately, a portion of humanity is still clear-headed and aware of the danger and is ready to defend our most precious values with all its strength.

In this global crisis, which seems to be a matter of the life or death for civilization, meditation and thought might be considered irrelevant or ineffective; the crisis seems to require the direct participation of everyone in this daily fight against an immediate enemy, not unlike soldiers in the trenches. However, invisible forces are at play behind concrete events, ideal factors that can only be combated by taking up the arms of thought. Contemporary philosophy has painstakingly tried to make contact with reality and take its place in the fight to serve human life and civilization. It understands the urgency of establishing an ideological front to oppose the errors that undermine the very basis of human existence itself. The themes discussed briefly in this book are not far from the vital problems that trouble the outlook of history today, as one might think given its abstractness. Whoever develops or explores the implications of these themes, however slightly, will be able to see how they relate to the most burning questions of daily experience.

The thesis that underwrites this book, which is perhaps to be read between the lines, is that the exterior events of life reflect the idea of what it means to be human, the consciousness or unconsciousness of our true destiny. History will be grand or petty depending on how great or small our estimation of our own values is. The thesis of this book was inspired by the eternal validity of the Socratic maxim, which says unto us: know thyself. A human being is not a mere product of history, dragged along like a lifeless corpse through the river of change. History is a human creation that reflects our strength and weakness, our heroism and small-mindedness. We and nothing else are responsible for our history. When we speak of major historical factors, such as the economy, do we mean to suggest that it is the work of nature? Is it not clear that every form of economy is an organization created by humans?

The science of history tells us that civilization is not the work of nature. On the contrary, as a result of our effort to elevate ourselves above our natural state to a form of existence independent of cosmic elements, it contrasts with nature. Modern biology, backed by ample evidence, has offered a new explanation of the relation between the individual and their environment, which has relegated the antiquated theory of "adaptation" to the far corner of useless junk. That theory was based on the presupposition of a "single environment" in which different species of animals fight for survival, a fight to the death out of which only the strongest and most fit for adaptation are victorious. Darwin's famous theory, which explained the evolution of biological species, carried over to the plane of human society and was appropriated by a materialist conception of history. The most recent developments in biology, without departing from a close observation of the facts, have demonstrated that Darwinism is false.[1] Living beings do not divide into the adaptable and unadaptable; they all possess a world they have adapted to. According to its peculiar sensibility, each species and every living being chooses and sets aside the set of objects that it needs to exist, and it forms its own world with them. What is modified is not the living being but the environment that surrounds it. The phenomenon unfolds in the opposite way described by Darwin: what adapts is the environment to the living being. With the support of science, these conclusions allow us to restore the autonomy and spontaneity of living beings in the face of the natural world that surrounds them, and to abandon the idea that differences in appearance are acquired merely under the pressure of external circumstances to which they must conform.

The autonomy and spontaneity common to all living beings reach their greatest perfection in the human being. Intelligence and genius have transformed nature into a civilization in which humans find all they need. Civilization is also a form of conquering nature that we have mastered progressively by means of reason and science. At the same time, it is a form of control that signifies freedom from the determinism that governs all natural phenomena. The fruit of this freedom, the greatest project of our creative power, is our spiritual culture. Whoever thinks of culture as the spirit's servitude to the material conditions of life ignores the fact, always confirmed by

---

1. [At the turn of the century, several non-Darwinian theories were developed to explain the source of new biological forms for which Darwinism offered no satisfactory explanation. One of the most successful of these theories was Henri Bergson's idea of a creative evolution. Bergson tried to explain the source of new genetic information from which natural selection can select. Bergson's theory postulated that all life emerges, not from mechanical forces, but from a vital impulse that causes evolution. Bergson's theory was awarded a Nobel Prize because at the time it appeared to be a plausible explanation of the source of genetic variety. When it was discarded, other theories, like orthogenesis and macromutations, were postulated. Both of them have also since been discounted. See Jerry Bergman, "Creative Evolution: An Anti-Darwin Theory Won a Nobel," *The Institute for Creation Research* (July 1, 2007); and Peter Bowler, *Charles Darwin: The Man and His Influence* (London: Blackwell Publishers, 1990).]

history, that culture is only produced by virtue of a relative freedom from such material conditions.

Historical materialism does not take into account that the economy is not a natural fact, but an integral part of civilization and therefore a human creation.[2] Though materialism has falsely interpreted this fact, it is undeniable that every form of culture somehow conveys the state of social reality in which it is produced. Culture must be nourished and supported by the concrete forces of society, and it is also clear that the products of culture opposed or not connected to the vital interests of the moment inevitably die out. The right interpretation of this fact is that material conditions negatively influence culture. Culture is entirely free to create products that are disconnected from their material conditions, but these products cannot survive in the absence of a vital atmosphere that nourishes them. Concerning the parallel between culture and the material conditions of a specific historical moment that does in fact exist ("structure" and "superstructure" in Marxism), this should be explained solely by the fact that the same spirit created both. Materialism takes the economy to be the primordial cause as if it were something given by nature prior to all human creation. But history shows, when observed without prejudice, that economics is not part of "nature" but of civilization, that is, it is a product of the human effort to modify natural conditions. If there is always a correspondence between an economic system and the contemporaneous culture, that is not because the forms of production and exchange are caused by a superstructure, but rather because both are the effect of the same cause. Although historical materialism thinks of the economy as the trunk and the rest of human functions as branches, the economy should be considered a branch and the human the trunk, with our changing mode of being. Now, the reasons for this change should be sought out in a law within the human, parallel to a cosmic rhythm, not from without. The

---

2. [Although Marxist philosophers had been expelled from the National University since the early 1930s, Marxism remained one of the most influential schools of thought during the twentieth century in Mexico. Among the most important representatives were Vicente Lombardo Toledano, Valentín Campa, and Hernán Laborde.]

human being changes because the primordial law of everything that exists is change, constant becoming.

The increasingly widespread consciousness of the central position of the human being has provoked the demand for a rigorous science, aimed especially at studying the human being, so as not to leave it to the whims of superficial studies without a firm philosophical foundation. The knowledge of the human being requires a special discipline that, taking advantage of the more established successes in epistemology, develops a method adequate to investigate its object systematically. In the body of this exposition, I have tried to define, in logical order, the problems and tasks of philosophical anthropology. They unfolded gradually, from establishing the principles or fundamental axioms of this science to arriving at a conception of the concrete human. There I pointed out the position of anthropology in relation to other special sciences concerning humans. I explained why the most well-established conclusions of anthropology must provide the guiding assumptions of sociology, law, ethics, etc. I also showed the privileged position of this new science in relation to philosophy. Here one needs only to recall the observation that there is an implicit presupposition concerning the human being in each of the various theories of knowledge.

In reaction to the naturalist conception of being human, philosophy today has restored certain values that are genuinely human, but it has done so this time on a positive basis. The notion of the spirit has reclaimed its autonomous rights against the denials of materialism. A new concept of freedom enables us to understand it as a real attribute of the human being without infringing upon the mechanical order of the universe. The philosophical justification of personality restores its rightful place to the human individual whom naturalism tried to dissolve into the masses or collectivity. But it is important to make clear that this new idea elevates the human without falling into the mistaken position of idealism and subjectivism, which attributes every class of laws to the subject until they become the "legislator of the universe." The laws of knowledge, morality, art, etc., were considered merely subjective relations. The originality of the new concept of the human rests on the recognition of an objective order of realities and values that support and provide norms of human functions. Whoever, passing superficial judgment, describes the theories of philosophical anthropology under the name of "spiritualism" does not understand them in the slightest. If philosophy today has reaffirmed the existence of the spirit, freedom, and personality, at bottom it has given these words a new meaning that bears no resemblance to the entities of traditional metaphysics.

The sciences have probably never before analyzed in such detail how human nature is composed, nor recognized the multiplicity of its ingredients, be they vital, psychic, social, etc. And yet never before have we understood that the essence of the human being cannot be reduced to any particular element, but can only be found in the constitutive unity of ingredients, in the being of the totality.

Never before has the affirmation of the unity of the human being been timelier because now, more than ever, the unity has been lost. The situation described in the first chapter shows that the disproportionate growth of a material and mechanical civilization threatens to annihilate authentic human values. Recent events reveal that the dominance of irrational forces in history persists in their destructive work. We are witnessing the most comprehensive reign of violence, passion, hate, so extreme that it has led civilized humanity to madness. Is the philosophical expression that affirms the values of the spirit romantic? It seems to me that the essence of philosophy is to stay calm and clear-headed in this moment of confusion and to take advantage of historical experience to show how, when our material efforts lack direction or spiritual control, they lead to destruction.

The human is neither a material being exclusively, nor a purely spiritual being. The spirit is consciousness, direction toward an end with value, an ideal trajectory, but it lacks the power of realization. A disembodied spirit would be utterly impotent. At every step history confirms that the spirit is a weak flame that the slightest breeze can put out. The spirit cannot live without the complement of material forces. Only the lower layers of the human being have the force, the power of realization, that the spirit on occasion can sublimate or channel in the direction of its goals. Everything the spirit achieves is the fruit of this cooperation of opposing elements: blind but energetic force, powerless but spiritual direction. The best moments in history are those in which those two sides of the human being are unified and act in concert. This unity of action constitutes human life proper. The opposite, that is, the separation of elements, signifies death. The disintegration of the human being is objectively manifest in history through the opposition and struggle between diverse entities in which each one of the elements is embodied without the rest. In general, it is the opposition between the intellectual and the vital or instinctual type—the struggle between young and old, between masculinity and femininity, between the masses and the elites, between the inferior and superior social classes, between culture and the barbaric in civilization. All these oppositions translate into various forms of antithesis between thought and life, so characteristic of our time. A very common irrationalist conviction assumes that the operative forces in history are blind instincts, unintelligent passions, in short, impulses that pulsate in the obscurity of the subconscious. The role assigned to the intellect is as a merely technical instrument that executes the decisions of an irrational will. Scientific knowledge is only a means for exploiting and dominating nature, as well as human energies. From this pragmatic opinion emerges, as a logical corollary, the devaluation of knowledge as objective truth. A powerful global movement has demoted the intellect by claiming that it is not the arbiter of action, and that the goal of being human is not to think and know but to live and work. In this way, the intellect is reduced to the secondary function of corroborating what has already been accomplished.

Irrationalism in politics leads to either of the following consequences: anarchy or dictatorship. A politics that does not accept the guidance of the intellect is a politics bereft of compass or wheel, drifting along in the wind. But irrationalist politics can also lead to the justification of brute force as the only norm of life. Thus, the perspectives offered along this path are in no way comforting: either disorder without feet or head, or order by means of violence, that is, dictatorship.

The point of view of the philosophy sketched out in this book is not to resolve the opposition in favor of one side, but to understand

and justify the rights belonging to each party in the conflict. Without reservation, it not only recognizes the value of vitality as the raw material and driving force of the human person, but, on the other hand, it also reveals that human existence would not be possible without the guidance and nobility of the spirit. Scheler says, "The human person is not a 'substance,' but a complex of actions organized monarchically, that is, a complex in which *one* act always guides and governs."

The old dispute between materialism and spiritualism cannot be settled partially in favor of one side alone. Philosophically we cannot speak of a soul that, in another life, might exist without a body, according to the view that Plato imparted to Western religious culture. But philosophically we also cannot maintain the negative theory that conceives of the human being as a body without a soul, be it the intelligent machine of the eighteenth-century materialist or the gregarious animal of the nineteenth-century naturalist.[3] The soul and body are not two isolated substances that do not communicate, as Cartesian dualism asserts, or substances whose union needs to be explained by a "preestablished harmony." Soul and body are two elements that interpenetrate in a way that constitutes a unity in the human being. If the same process is looked at from the outside, it appears to be a physiological phenomenon; looked at from the inside, a psychological phenomenon. However, as described in the first chapter, a vicious view of the human was on the verge of destroying the unity of our being, pitting material values against spiritual values. The only thing that philosophy can try to do is demonstrate that this internal division is not a necessary law of human existence, but an accident of history. Perhaps in the future the pain caused by the internal conflict will lead us toward the synthesis of antagonistic forces, toward the reestablishment of harmony, first in one's individual being and then in their historical existence. Let us hope that Scheler was right in thinking that we should not oppose this ideal of unification because it represents a fate that will lead to the future realization of the integral human being.

---

3. [See "The Preoccupation with Death" in the related writings.]

RELATED WRITINGS

A Conception of Culture[1]
August 1925

Not every expression that travels by word of mouth owes its circulation to the fact that its meaning is precise and widely understood. Some words slip into everyday usage *because* they are vague and mean something different to everyone. Such is the case, for example, with the word *culture*. Since nobody knows exactly what it means, anyone can invent their own meaning, often mistaken or even absurd. It's a neat trick that some people use to convince others that they know what they're talking about. To the imaginary enemy, they telegraph in advance the defects of culture that will lead to its ruin.

Roughly, common sense understands culture to mean that a person is well-read in the sciences, literature, history, etc. The cultured person is one who has "knowledge," that is, the learned one; or one who "is well-informed," that is, the erudite individual. And if such a person did represent culture, then it would deserve the condemnation of its enemies.

Culture would then not be a property inherent in the spirit, but a qualifier added by the possession of cultural goods. In that case, it would be defined as a relation of ownership. And just as the owner and the object owned exist apart as two distinct things, the spirit would exist as one thing, the culture possessed as another. Deep down the cultured individual would think, feel, and desire as the uncultured

---

1. "The Concept of Culture" is a section of a slightly longer essay titled, "By Way of a Prologue," published for the first issue of the second volume of *La Antorcha*. Samuel Ramos, "A guisa de prólogo," in *Obras Completas*, vol. 1 (México City: Universidad Autónoma de México, 1975), 255–59. Throughout the Related Writings, all notes are the translator's.

individual does. But it doesn't work like this because the uncultured person's "culture," as a foreign body, prevents them from all spontaneous movement.

However, that is not culture; it is not a property that is in the spirit and at the same time foreign to it. It is not a quality juxtaposed to the individual. Culture is a substantial quality of the spirit; the relation between the spirit and culture is not that of content and container; one does not have culture "in" the spirit; the spirit "is" cultured.

Of course, culture can be acquired even without the superficial memory with which the student learns how to conjugate verbs. One is not cultured for remembering phrases, paragraphs, or entire books verbatim; culture is not a quantitative change to memory, but a qualitative change to spirit. Each lesson, then, ought to be a vital experience that stirs the entire soul; each vital experience ought to be a lesson. Ideas or books might not leave a well-defined stamp on the memory; but, for the sake of enriching culture, they ought to leave a profound stamp on one's entire being. Each step of one's education should result in a change in one's feelings, ideas, tastes. The cultured individual does not act as the vulgar person does, and for that reason they might be called extravagant. But they are sincere: what they do is aligned with how they feel and think. They are not phony like someone pretending to be cultured. In the end, someone who counterfeits culture is a mongrel [*un mestizo*] who doesn't work as hard as the vulgar person because they believe they are cultured, nor do they feel as the cultured person does.

The enemies of culture think that someone in the state of nature is superior to the cultured individual. The former has a more realistic and spontaneous view of nature, while the latter has distorted it with the contrivances of culture. This attitude is justified if what is being compared is someone of artificial culture. But true culture, in the sense here given, is synonymous with perfection, and it should therefore be said that someone is cultured insofar as they have a more penetrating view of reality than the primitive human being; a consciousness more refined, more sensible, and consequently better able to understand life; culture doesn't impede someone from communicating with the external world. On the contrary, it is progress toward realism.

This raises a serious question concerning the acquisition of culture: How much time is required to cultivate a consciousness [of culture]? Is the span of an individual life sufficient? Human experience confirms that the evolution of the spirit is slow. Perfection is not achieved even over the course of generations; each generation destroys part of what the previous generation has achieved. Each new being does not begin living where the other leaves off. Everyone who aspires to a high degree of perfection, even if not total perfection, has to recreate the history of culture, as the embryo reproduces in brief the history of the species. Heredity never passes on specific traits. Nobody is born knowing how to speak. Everyone has to learn the language of their parents from scratch. Life begins anew for each being. Perhaps the only benefit of heredity is that it gradually decreases the amount of time it takes for the individual to acquire the history that they must repeat. The greatest capacity of a consciousness consists, then, in inheriting the ability to develop at a faster pace.

After the Great War, which destroyed the illusion of progress once and for all, it is clear that heredity does nothing for human improvement. Thus, according to Bernard Shaw, man is small to the extent that life is short. The only solution is longevity. All hope rests on being able to go *back to Methuselah*.

Max Scheler
Hipótesis [1928][1]

To someone unfamiliar with contemporary philosophical literature it may be difficult to imagine that the most essential human problems might be treated under the heading "knowledge and culture." But, in a lengthy speech bearing this title, recently published in *La Revista de Occidente*, this is what Scheler does. A sweeping philosophy, rich in thought, is condensed into a few short pages, which are enough to get a sense of the author's breadth. Scheler is considered a first-rate philosopher in Germany. In truth, among Germany's abundant intellectual output, works of such "grand style," such as Scheler's philosophy that can be gleaned from the book we are about to consider, are uncommon. Indeed, aside from their theoretical content, his ideas capture an *ethos* that, with the powerful virtue of lifting us up, reveal in the act a soaring thinker. His text brings to mind a certain distinction made by Vasconcelos: "Books that one reads standing and books that one reads sitting."[2] Naturally, the books that lift us out of our seat are essential books. It would be very difficult to completely sum up a work that is itself a breviary of philosophy, a work in which no concept is subordinate, and in which every phrase is bursting with meaning. But I will not resist the temptation to share the most important thoughts in the book, which is not an easy read, underscoring along the way ideas that I believe deserve further thought.

The simplistic idea that culture is acquired out of aesthetic interest arises from dilettantism—that is, the idea that culture lends elegance to a person's interiority in the way a suit lends it to the body. Scheler objects to this dandyism and affirms, instead, the ethical significance

---

1. In Ramos, *Obras Completas*, vol. 1, 52–57.
2. The essay Ramos is referring to, "Books I Read Sitting and Books I Read Standing," is published in English in José Vasconcelos, *The Modern Mexican Essay*, ed. José Luis Martínez, trans. H. W. Hilborn (Toronto: University of Toronto Press, 1975), 97–100.

of culture.[3] It is not surprising that these two, ethics and culture, are combined into a single problem. What is surprising, rather, is that they are ever separated. It is difficult to see how someone uncultured, that is, someone without personality, might possess ethical value. Because, above all, as Scheler says, "culture is therefore a category of being"; its process is just what is called the perfection of spirit. On the other hand, no one who is conscious of their spiritual elevation ever wants to live at odds with oneself. I am convinced that only one thing is necessary in morality: to feel aligned with one's own personality (or, in other words, that each fulfills their destiny). Last year, in a provisional article, I defined culture as *something that one is, not something that one has*. Scheler now confirms this opinion for me when he says that "culture is a category of being, not of knowledge or experience."[4] At another point, he explains that the cultured person is "the one who has acquired in the world a *personal structure*, an inclusive concept of ideally mobile patterns superimposed on each other, in order to arrive at *one single* way to view the world, to think, comprehend, judge, and deal with the world and *all* of its fortuitous manifestations—patterns *anterior* to fortuitous experience, capable of utilizing and integrating this experience into the entity of their personal '*world*.'"[5]

It should be added that, even though personality is the most radical form of existing in opposition to the world—given that we are persons only when we feel completely different from it, and only when we acquire freedom, that is, the power to separate ourselves from the common destiny of inferior beings in order to follow a unique destiny—personality cannot grow or expand without making contact with the world. Thus, Scheler declares that anyone who does not participate in what there essentially is in the world cannot make

---

3. By "dandyism," Scheler is referring to the desire to make oneself into a work of art, a kind of "egocentric self-planning, be it of one's own beauty, virtue, form, or knowledge." Max Scheler, "The Forms of Knowledge and Culture," 31. The purpose of culture is not to perfect oneself through an act of sheer will. Instead, "only the man willing to *lose* himself in a noble cause or in some kind of true companionship, unafraid of what might be the outcome, will *win himself*," 32.
4. Scheler, "The Forms of Knowledge and Culture," 19.
5. Scheler, "The Forms of Knowledge and Culture," 47.

themselves cultured. Culture then is a phenomenon with two faces, and it is advisable to look at it from both sides to avoid any suspicion of individualism.

What is commonly understood by human morality? The term *morality* is applied when it teaches one how to achieve their destiny on Earth. But it reveals an end to human activity outside and distinct from itself. It believes that the individual should work—even sacrifice one's life if necessary—for justice, liberty, culture, etc. I don't wish to deny that these ideals stimulate moral conduct, but it is easily forgotten that they are only pretexts for revealing personality. Is it unreasonable to suppose that these ideals are not valuable in themselves but because they benefit human beings? Some might say that this is obvious and not worth pointing out. However, what is most simple and obvious is obscured by the assumption that the most important truths should be complicated and difficult. It might seem ridiculous to employ philosophical technique to prove common sense. But it is necessary: sometimes the task of the philosopher is to sweep away the prejudice that obstructs a clear vision of things, restoring the mind to its primitive state. One is then surprised for not having seen the truth right in front of them. In the strict sense, morality can only be called human when it recognizes that the human being's ultimate end is the human being. The Bible says, "The Sabbath was made for man, not man for the Sabbath."[6] However, according to many moral philosophers, "Man was made for the Sabbath"; that is, human life is bereft of moral value and has to be put in the service of certain goods (justice, culture, etc.) so that one might receive the radiation of their goodness.

One of the more reassuring aspects of Scheler's philosophy is his authentic humanism. He insistently extols the intrinsic value of the human being, considering the human the ideal fruit of existence, as "the meaning of the earth, indeed, of the world itself."[7] As a matter of fact, this idea can already be found in Kant's moral philosophy, but it goes unnoticed or is downplayed in philosophical commentaries.

---

6. Mark 2:27. See "A New Humanism" in this volume.
7. Scheler, "The Forms of Knowledge and Culture," 30.

Otto Weininger was one of the few who recognized its importance and how to wield it in his admirable outline of ethics. Today, Scheler is the only philosopher who has returned to this idea and who has, on the basis of it, produced an original study of culture. The human being was not made for culture, but culture for the human, or, according to the formula of the German philosopher: "Culture is humanization." To make use of culture, one need only answer the following question: What is "the human being"? Scheler's treatment of this subject is one of the most novel and appealing features of the book we are analyzing. He inquires into the essence of the human being, comparing it to that of animals. And by making use of the latest developments in physiology and psychology, he arrives at unexpected conclusions.

The human being is characterized, from the scientific point of view, *by the brain*. (Anatomically speaking, the human is the "most cerebral" being, complete with a frontal lobe. Physiologically speaking, the brain is an organ that consumes enormous amounts of energy and lives off the rest of the body; this makes humans a "veritable slave to the brain.") At the same time, "The cortex is *least* able to recuperate, least capable of phylogenesis." Thus, what is properly human, the brain, is the greatest hindrance to the development of the human being. The vital process has been stagnated in that organ. Thus, "the species man is *least* likely to evolve." "Superman, in the biological sense, is a fairy tale." In order to be conserved in the human species, life was transformed into spirit. But from the point of view of natural science, the history of humanity shows that through this detour humans have barely achieved what the animal achieves automatically guided by instinct. Nor are practical intelligence and technology exclusive to humans; the animal also has them.[8]

What, then, distinguishes human beings from other animals? For Scheler, humans are characterized by their "capacity to act *autonomously* in the face of all psychic, vital causality (including practical intelligence governed by drives), a causality no longer analogous and parallel to the functional process of the nervous system, but parallel

---

8. This paragraph is a loose paraphrase of "The Forms of Knowledge and Culture," 23–24.

and analogous to the *objective structure of objects and values in the world itself*."[9] In this paragraph Scheler declares that what is specific to human beings is our capacity to develop our psychic life according to a law independent of nature. And, as we suggested earlier, we do not need to understand autonomy as the isolation of the individual from the world. In order to grow physically and psychically, humans must nourish themselves, and can only find the sustenance they need in the world. The vulgar person is dragged down by the influence of the natural world, and thereby is not free. They are the product of the general laws that govern inferior creatures. Indeed, the principle of freedom consists in opposing itself to these laws; but it is not a principle of anarchy. The meaning of the word *freedom* is unclear. For one to subscribe [to the principle] of freedom, in theory, it is not necessary to deny determinism. Subscribing to the thesis of freedom only requires the belief that the world obeys more than one causal chain of events, and that, in addition to the most extensive of them all, the natural, there exist other independent series: the destiny of each individual. As inhabitants of the natural world, individuals must first overthrow the predominance of their energies. Then, to arouse the formation of their own being, they must open their psyche to the influence of external values. The world can be the determinant cause of our spiritual growth when we present it to ourselves under any of these three aspects: the aesthetic, philosophical, and moral. The function of culture is precisely to draw out and represent these diverse values of the world. And a work is cultural only when it is capable of stimulating and exalting human spirituality. Science, for example, is indifferent to values; from its point of view, everything that exists is of the same importance. Scientifically, the physical and the psychological are on the same plane. The evaluation of these phenomena is the subject of philosophy. And insofar as science does not take value into account, it lacks cultural force.

The sole essence of culture and its philosophical justification is *humanization*. "Each historical activity cultivates not in goods, artistic achievements, not in the unending extension of knowledge through

---

9. "The Forms of Knowledge and Culture," 28.

the experimental sciences, but in this well and nobly created *being of man*, in his *collaboration in realizing God*."[10] According to Scheler, for now this spiritual human being exists only as an idea: he writes, "[man is] an eternal *task* and eternally resplendent objective for man as a living creature."[11]

Based on the previous considerations, Scheler arrives at the conclusion, important for discrediting the *dilettanti* once and for all: culture is not a good available to just anyone; it is not achieved voluntarily. Culture is "mission, destiny"; the individuals who are predisposed to it go about realizing it in every act of their lives—not just by reading—"it takes place behind the back of mere intent and mere will."[12] Such individuals, however, employ external resources to stimulate culture. But these resources are of such a nature that, as the same philosopher shows, they are rarely within reach.

"The first and most important (positive stimuli to culture) appears to be the *example of worth we discover in a person* who has won our love and admiration. *At least once* the *entire* man must have been in something whole, pure, free, noble [if he wants to become 'cultured']."[13] Here we have, in my view, one of Scheler's more important theories. How well it explains certain historical phenomena in Spanish America! Why do our cultural ventures almost always produce such mediocre results? Because the instruments at our disposal are, exclusively, *works* of culture; our scarcity of cultured *persons* is alarming. Herein lies, for example, the problem of higher education that, for us, is a problem of persons. There is certainly an objective culture that is more or less within everyone's reach. But the idea that it is effective in itself goes too far. If someone believes that anyone can put to use a clear, simple, and even well-timed idea about morality, education, and politics, they are mistaken. What tremendous vibrancy the very same

---

10. "The Forms of Knowledge and Culture," 31.
11. "The Forms of Knowledge and Culture," 25. The translation of "living creature" is *hombre-naturaleza*, a hyphenated term that emphasizes that by "living" Ramos includes being "part of nature."
12. "The Forms of Knowledge and Culture," 31.
13. "The Forms of Knowledge and Culture," 33.

idea acquires when it is stirred up by someone with great personal gifts recognized by everyone. Let us warm up to the idea that in order to solve our problems in education, planning is not enough; what is needed are theories in the hands of *uniquely* qualified individuals.[14]

To cultivate oneself by means of knowledge is to "transform the *material* of knowledge into *force* for knowledge; that is, it is a true functional growth of the spirit itself in the process of knowledge." There is no "knowledge for the sake of knowledge"; that does not make any sense. The aim of knowledge is to modify the spirit of the one who knows, and also, through this, to change the world. When we want to make use of the world by means of knowledge [*conocimiento*], we produce scientific knowledge [*saber*]. If we want to develop spiritual life, we do philosophy; I have already explained that philosophy represents *knowledge of culture*. And, finally, knowledge ascends to the rank of *knowledge of salvation* when it is presented to influence how the world unfolds.

According to Scheler, these are the three forms of knowledge. "In the past, each great civilization has developed the three kinds of knowledge in a one-sided fashion. India has cultivated knowledge of salvation. . . . China and Greece championed knowledge of culture. The Occident, since the beginning of the twelfth century, has emphasized the knowledge of work of experimental, specialized science."[15] Pure scientific knowledge is especially impotent in the effort to achieve human perfection. The greatest development of science might very well leave humans spiritually empty, even in a stage of complete barbarism. That is why the German philosopher makes his case, because in his future, humanity will integrate the three forms of knowledge.

In conclusion, what stands out the most in Scheler's philosophy is his authentic sense of humanism—the idea that the human being is the meaning of the whole of existence. An idea that, given its sheer simplicity, one might be inclined to call primitive. And, in effect, it is.

---

14. Such as José Vasconcelos. See Ramos's "Twenty Years of Education in Mexico."
15. "The Forms of Knowledge and Culture," 48.

However, having lost our way among an accumulation of the prejudices of civilization, it is now time for a philosophical mind to remove them, and convince others that it is the only ethical principle that is self-evident. At the same time, the concept of culture will be saved if we define it as a process of humanization; in this way, culture is clearly different from various other things that, not being culture, have nevertheless served as the basis to condemn it. A range of goods created by material civilization or the work of a certain species of artificial souls have been mistaken for culture. But who will dare to condemn culture once one is convinced that it is not defined by the acquisition of the goods just mentioned, but by the inevitable purification of the person who has the will to value for its own sake, thereby realizing their spiritual essence. These notes would remain incomplete if they did not make mention of Scheler's pronounced religious orientation. He affirms that fate indicates an aim beyond the human being, who, that said, carries in their breast the seed of the divine. Over the course of history, God is born little by little. Thus, when we make ourselves cultured, we surpass our essence and are deified.

The Mechanization of Human Life[1]

Without a doubt, mechanism [*el maquinismo*][2] is one of the more notorious features of the present age, and although it has not completely swept over every country around the world, its sphere of influence increases daily in every direction. In countries like ours, it has displaced unnumberable primitive means of production that, little by little, give way to the victorious drive of the modern machine. With the exception of the indigenous peasant, who refuses to give up their traditional tools despite the clear superiority of modern tools, Mexicans admire the latter and are happy to employ them. Everyone who loves strength and power enthusiastically champions the machine, which represents the tangible materialization of the power that their will desires. But it is clear that the true value of the machine lies in its utility, in simplifying work and saving energy that, in theory, it should produce. I say "in theory" because we ought to ask whether in practice machines haven't made life more complicated, or whether we haven't created a monster that will eventually devour us.

In any event, in Mexico, as in almost every other Latin American country, the rise of mechanism is enjoying favorable conditions, and perhaps in the not-so-distant future, we will find ourselves on par with the more civilized countries on Earth. Eventually, the entire world will be covered with machines. The machine is like a universal language understood at every latitude by people of every country and race. If a global catastrophe were to destroy civilization, machines would represent for future humanity—should it exist—what monstrous animals of the tertiary age represent to us. Their museums will exhibit the remains of steel monsters, and our entire history, complicated and laborious, will be reduced to the following heading: "The age of the machine."

---

1. Published in *Hoy*, no. 78, August 20, 1938.
2. See chapter 1, fn. 5 in the main text.

It is not surprising that, surrounded by machines, our manner of being would take something from theirs, or that one would begin to consider oneself and the surrounding world a machine. As the unfolding of modern life is still underway, and because humanity is beset by numerous problems and difficulties, some plans to resolve them amount to imposing on society a mechanical structure. A dictatorial regime, for example, can succeed only if it converts individuals into mechanical units incapable of moving on their own, but only by a force that the dictator transmits to the whole mechanism from above. The vital organs of society, industry, commerce, etc., are made to function like clockwork. The assumption today is that the only way to successfully run a business, industry, or even the national economy and the whole of social life, is according to a scientific plan. What is called scientific organization consists in trying to make that which is being organized function exactly like a machine. It assumes that any other form of organization is inferior and doesn't yield results on the same scale as the scientific. One might now begin to image what a society scientifically organized might look like.

First, the State would encroach upon every sphere of life, leaving nothing beyond its influence. This is already happening in fascist countries and in Russia, where the way of organizing and operating the State are identical and differ only in their ideological content. It is clear that this invasion of the State completely annuls individual freedom. All mechanical organization must be imposed by force, impersonally, and it considers the characteristics that distinguish us, the nuances of individuality, harmful to collective life. Ideally, individuals would be made the same, as though they were cast from the same mold. The individual disappears in the anonymous mass and becomes a numerical unit in a fixed series. Presumably, absolute uniformity cannot be achieved unless the State can regulate procreation, diet, and education according to scientific principles that turn people into a serial product, like cars or fountain pens.

Without arriving at such extremes, the modern human being is already mechanized, simply for having lived among machines, which one has to operate and look after constantly. [Hermann von]

Keysserling [*sic*] has said that the person who best represents our age is the *chauffeur*. It should be added that the greatest modern superstition is the faith in technique, and the increased technification is steering us toward complete mechanization. By a strange paradox, we who created machines to serve us, must now serve them. How many people work and toil more than before in order to buy cars or radios that, in most cases, are not indispensable to their lives! Perhaps the day will come when such machines, along with fashionable others, will become absolutely necessary to life, like the telephone, and then human beings will have a new master to serve. But what is truly incomprehensible is that people, obsessed with mechanism, would forfeit all human characteristics in order to transform the world in which they live into a mechanized system. In the name of what, then, would they employ scientific technique to organize future society? If in the name of well-being and happiness, they would be sorely mistaken. Even if a perfect world might one day be achieved, liberty, love, feelings—in sum, all that gives life value—would have to disappear. Such a world is naturally only a utopia, but someone once observed that real life aims at the realization of utopias. We used to think of utopias as unrealizable dreams, so they did not trouble us much. But now, we are forced to think about how to keep them from becoming a reality. Undoubtedly, human life would be perfect if it were organized scientifically and ran like a watch. But what does it matter if human life is not absolutely perfect, or so well ordered, if, in exchange, we are able to find more love and happiness?[3]

I don't mean to suggest that mechanical civilization is harmful in every way. Who knows if the blame is to fall on civilization itself or on those who have not figured out how to extract the beneficial

---

3. See William Barrett, *The Illusion of Technique: A Search for Meaning in a Technological Civilization* (Garden City: Anchor Books, 1979). Barrett writes: "So we would hope too that a highly technical civilization might still be able at some point to set aside its logical adherence to its techniques in order that it might possibly learn to live and love.... An example: Even if such research as that of Masters and Johnson on sex were to be made technically and logically perfect, one would hope that civilization were able to say, 'Yes, but it misses the point'" (111).

elements it contains. My aim is to highlight one of the evils that afflicts us today related to the environment created by the extreme degree of technical civilization. We often hear that we are becoming increasingly inhuman, and that there are many causes for this transformation. Above all, the inhabitants of modern cities, entangled in a web of artificial necessities and demands, likewise become artificial beings as their existence becomes increasingly distant from the sources of authentic life. As civilization progresses, there are fewer occasions to satisfy authentically human needs. Commitments multiply, work becomes more strenuous and grueling, it is necessary to live faster, and there is barely enough time to rest. Exhausted, one cannot enjoy life even during fleeting moments of leisure. One doesn't even have time to reflect on their sad existence, and if one has the good fortune of finally retiring from work, it is too late because they are too old.

Many seek to compensate for what is wrong with their existence, even though they are not aware exactly what that is. The enthusiasm for primitive life today is one sign of the discontent of civilized people.[4] Today there is a widespread desire for a simpler life, one free of complications and closer to Nature. Interest in the biographies of exceptional individuals is a kind of revenge of the mass-person, who has lost their personality beneath the leveling steamroller of civilization.[5] Perhaps one of the things that one desires most, though no one would dare confess this, is the ability to distinguish oneself from the masses and acquire their own personality. Finding one's personality,

---

4. In the original, parts of the first two sentences of this paragraph are inverted, so that it reads: "Muchos hombres, sin que logren precisar exactamente en donde está la falla de su existencia, tienden a El entusiasmo que hoy despierta la procurarse ciertas compensaciones. vida primitiva, es uno de los signos de la inconformidad del hombre civilizado." The translator has taken the liberty of making sense out of the paragraph that he is confident is a typographic error. Here Ramos is likely referring to *primitivism*, as represented in Picasso's "Les Demoiselles d'Avignon," Stravinsky's *The Rite of Spring*, the novels of D. H. Lawrence and Joseph Conrad, and T. S. Eliot's "The Hollow Men."

5. This is likely a reference to Kierkegaard's *The Present Age*.

realizing its values, is one form of compensation urgently called for at this time.

Outside of the City, where the artifices of modern civilization have already begun to be felt, our country has not yet been completely overtaken by the dehumanization found in more advanced countries. We are still quite close to Nature and to primitive existence. Here the problem seems to be the reverse: that of harnessing civilization to elevate the level of collective life. But precisely because we are at the beginning of this undertaking, it would be wise to consider the risks of civilization in order to prevent its potential evils. It would be absurd just to accept that mechanical civilization is here to impose upon us a new form of slavery and destroy life's most precious values. If the greater part of humanity today endures the slavery of physical work, why not make the machine the slave of the future and thereby turn it into a great instrument of human liberation?

A New Humanism[1]

In the section of *Hoy* titled "Book Reviews," Don Mariano Alcocer wrote a kind review of my book, *The Profile of Man and Culture in Mexico*, citing one of its conclusions at the end: we ought to return to humanism. But he quickly asks which humanism I'm referring to, perhaps because it has never been clear what the word means. After the publication of my book, though independent of it, much has been written on the subject of a new humanism both in America and Europe. I then realized that I had unintentionally hit upon a timely question, perhaps because intellectually something was in the air.

At first glance, mention of humanism today might seem outdated, and the attempt to revive it, artificial. Humanism was a large-scale literary and ideological movement that brought about cultural reform in the Renaissance. At the time, the so-called humanists were thought to be revolutionaries, the spokesmen of modernity. Humanism, however, was in itself a return to the past, a past more distant than the one they were trying to overcome. Through the legacy of its culture, they discovered the Greco-Latin world in its spiritual authenticity, made directly intelligible through the study of classical languages. However, what attracted them to the artifacts of Greece or Rome was not a taste for archaeology, but a living spirit of perennial significance that was made manifest for the first time in the Renaissance. Those artifacts contained in definitive form a sense of life similar to what was beginning to awaken in the new historical consciousness of the time. It was the concept of life that Nietzsche would describe centuries later as "the meaning of Earth."[2]

The Renaissance discovered that the obsession with otherworldly existence prevented human beings from caring and attending to their real life—their worldly existence. Humanism was a spiritual

---

1. Published in *Hoy*, no. 93, December 3, 1938.
2. A version of this paragraph is included in the "Prologue to the Third Edition" on p. 13 of the *Profile*.

movement to bring human beings from heaven down to earth, to confine their thought and action to the limits of reality, adjusting those limits to the reach of what is humanly possible.[3] That is how Humanism became the dominant system of education in European schools, persisting today through the study of dead languages that provide access to the life that pulsates in ancient texts. I do not know to what extent the humanities continue to fulfill their original purpose. Perhaps they have lost their early spontaneity and novelty and have become, over time, an antiquated discipline preserved solely by the prestige of tradition, having lost their founding spirit. But my aim here is not to question whether the classical humanities retain their educational value in the new conditions of life, since that is not the Humanism I am referring to in my book.

Simply put, we might say that whereas classical Humanism was a movement downward from above, the new Humanism ought to appear as a movement in exactly the opposite direction, that is, upward from below. That is what the new times require of it. In our modern civilization, there is a multitude of factors that have dragged human beings down to the level of subhumanity. Everything to counterbalance this descent is losing strength, and the fall accelerates unimpeded. One need not be a perceptive observer of current events to notice traits of subhumanity developing within us. Across a variety of daily occurrences, it is easy to see that human beings possess a will to sink into barbarism and savagery. As I write these lines, I read in the daily papers that among educated Germans of pure Aryan blood, the mob has given in to an excess of violence, such as arson and looting, that one would have thought were only possible among third- or fourth-class races.

Mexico is a young country, and youth is an ascendent force. In this fact, I see the guarantee that our will spontaneously tends toward elevating the quality of the human being, to the improvement of life, and, in general, to the development of all national potential. I have

---

3. For a sweeping overview of the varieties of humanism beginning in the Renaissance, see Sarah Bakewell, *Humanly Possible: Seven Hundred Years of Humanist Freethinking, Inquiry, and Hope* (New York: Penguin Press, 2023).

pointed out certain vices and defects in the Mexican psyche; nevertheless, I am convinced that a better destiny awaits us, that the future is ours. Our errors might be youthful errors that maturity will correct. Our psychology is that of a race at the age of fantasy and illusion, for which we will endure failure until we achieve an accurate sense of reality. I believe in the salvation of Mexico because our race lacks neither intelligence nor vitality; we only need to learn. However, the wisdom required is not learned in the classroom, but is the kind of wisdom an individual gains with great effort through trial and error. Here I am referring to the science of living, which is not found in books, but learned only through life itself. Like swimming, it can only be learned by jumping in, that is, by swimming. Until now, Mexicans have known only how to die; now it is necessary to substitute the wisdom of death for the wisdom of life.[4]

I have no doubt that the majority of changes and reforms undertaken in Mexico originate from a sincere will to improve, demonstrating the urge to make progress. But mixed in with these are other unconscious urges that distort and annul what is good about that desire. Psychoanalysis helps to uncover the dark forces in the Mexican soul that, disguised as aspirations for noble ends, prefer debasement. Often, simply out of hidden resentment or hate, false values are put before authentic values. At other times, the foreigner is blindly imitated, thereby suppressing native potential. Conversely, foreign values absent in Mexico are occasionally rejected in the name of a healthy intent to nationalize, even though it only conceals an absolute emptiness. But among these negative forces, the irrational impulse to imitate still seems to dominate, expressing itself in a puerile impatience to skip over the stages of development, like adolescents who smoke, not so much out of an early proclivity to vice, but because they imagine that with cigarette in mouth, they are fully formed adults.

I have resisted the seduction of foreign ideas and systems because they do not respond to the true needs of the country, and they might work against the nobler impulses of the Mexican soul. All ideas or

---

4. The following paragraphs were reprinted, almost verbatim, in the "Prologue to the Third Edition" in the *Profile*, 10–12.

political regimes that seek to turn the human being into a herd animal annul our freedom. Every form of materialism that conceives of the human as a purely instinctive being, reducing our psychological functions to biological needs (be they the desire for sex, food, or power), are forces that lead to sub-humanity. If we add to these the powerful influence of modern civilization that tends to mechanize life and turn the human into an automaton, we get a sense of the magnitude of factors that conspire to degrade human nature.

The problem is that these negative forces operate unconsciously, creating the illusion that individuals are pursuing progressive and regenerative ideals, even when the opposite is true. That is why, as a guiding principle in defense of the human being, it is necessary to expose them. Human values ought to be rescued, whatever the cost, from adverse forces that threaten to destroy them. At this moment, these are the reasons that justify establishing a new Humanism that, unlike classical Humanism, will proceed upward from below, demonstrating that the authentic human values transcend mere animality.

Ortega y Gasset and Spanish America[1]

Since Independence, philosophy in Hispano-American countries has reflected the style of thinking in European countries, which then represented the vanguard of ideas.[2] For political reasons, our countries broke away spiritually from Spain and we were no longer concerned with whether they had any ideas worthy of interest. It was only after 1920 that Spain regained its intellectual significance in Hispanic America, right as the desire for own original thought had awakened. As for Mexico, one might say that the desire to create a national philosophy, increasingly widespread, had existed for a long time. Much experience, the entirety of the last century, has taught us that imitating foreign ideas is not an innocent game, and that, more than once, it has led to painful and bloody national conflicts. But the practice of imitating is so deeply rooted that the threat of repeating the same mistake continues to exist. However, this proclivity for imitation is aggressively resisted by the aspiration, which has been developing for some time, to discover ourselves and construct our own world of ideas using domestic materials. Why does this remain an aspiration and why haven't we seen any results yet? Is the Mexican mind not sufficiently up to the task? I don't think this is the explanation for why we need but lack a national philosophy. Admittedly, this is one of the most difficult objectives one can set out to achieve. I suspect that the prospect of undertaking this work might scare off many. Perhaps others will merely smile and secretly pity the naivete of discussing such things. But, while acknowledging the difficulty of this undertaking, at the bottom of this attitude is a lack of confidence in oneself, an

---

1. Published in *Hoy*, no. 96, December 28, 1938.

2. In this paragraph, Ramos uses the word *pensamiento* [thought], not *filosofía*, as in the phrase "philosophy in Hispano-American countries." In this context, it is clear that he is talking about philosophy, but it is worth pointing out that *pensamiento* is broader in meaning and suggests that he is operating with an understanding of philosophy that is not purely academic or professional.

inferiority complex that inhibits the inspiration for personal creation. If we decided just to start, we might discover at the outset that the undertaking is not as impossible as it seems.

Moreover, a lack of confidence would almost certainly try to defend itself by presenting theoretical arguments that conclude that the call for a national philosophy is self-contradictory. If by "national philosophy" we are referring to a body of true beliefs about Mexican reality and the surrounding world, which we try to obtain from our point of view, one might object, first of all, that knowledge is "impersonal." In other words, what is true in Paris, London, and Berlin is also true in Mexico, and vice versa. Therefore, if science and philosophy already exist in Europe,[3] they ought to be valid and apply to the particular case of Mexico, because the truth they contain is true everywhere. As it happens, philosophy and the sciences are studied in the classroom and university without taking into consideration their place of origin and considering only their truths in the abstract. While there is no doubt that the principles of knowledge and general laws of Nature are universal, individuals can have personal and varied perspectives of the same object. This is the problem where I think a few of Ortega y Gasset's key ideas enter to clear away the confusion and convince us that a national philosophy is not only a real possibility, but is even the only authentic way to think. In my view, herein lies the value and importance of the Spanish philosopher for Mexico and the Continent more broadly: the affirmation that all knowledge involves a perspective.

Ortega y Gasset, regarded today as an important European philosopher, has initiated and inspired a bona fide intellectual renaissance in Spain, which has had a profound impact across the American Continent. Exceptionally well-written, his books develop a personal doctrine whose ideological roots can be traced back to contemporary German philosophy. In his first book, *Meditations on Quixote*, he presents a theory of reality and of philosophy. In this work, Ortega teaches us that the whole conception of the world is a perspective presented to a particular thinker. He writes, "When shall we open

---

3. Here Ramos uses *filosofía*.

our minds to the conviction that the ultimate reality of the world is neither matter nor spirit, is no definite thing, but a perspective? God is perspective and hierarchy; Satan's sin was an error of perspective."[4] "Cosmic reality is such that it can only be seen in a single definite perspective. Perspective is one of the component parts of reality. Far from being a disturbance of its fabric, it is its organizing element. A reality which remained the same from whatever point of view it was observed would be a ridiculous conception."[5] "Two men may look, from different view-points, at the same landscape. Yet they do not see the same thing. Their different situations make the landscape assume two distinct types of organic structure in their eyes. The part which, in the one case, occupies the foreground, and is thrown into high relief in all its details, is, in the other case, the background, and remains obscure and vague in its appearance. Further, inasmuch as things which are put one behind the other are either wholly or partially concealed, each of the two spectators will perceive portions of the landscape which elude the attention of the other. Would there be any sense in either declaring the other's view of the landscape false? Evidently not; the one is as real as the other. But it would be just as senseless if, when our spectators found that their views of the landscape did not agree, they concluded that both views were illusory. Such a conclusion would involve belief in the existence of a third landscape, an authentic one, not subject to the same conditions as the other two. Well, an archetypal landscape of this kind does not and cannot exist."[6] "This way of thinking leads to a radical reform in philosophy, and also, which is more important, to a reform in our sensuous reaction to the cosmos."[7]

"Every life is a point of view directed upon the universe. Strictly speaking, what one life sees no other can. Every individual, whether

---

4. José Ortega y Gasset, *Meditations on Quixote* (New York: W. W Norton & Company 1961 [1914]), 44–45.

5. José Ortega y Gasset, *The Modern Theme*, trans. James Cleugh (New York: Harper Torchbooks, 1961), 90.

6. Ortega y Gasset, *The Modern Theme*, 89–90.

7. Ortega y Gasset, *The Modern Theme*, 90.

person, nation or epoch, is an organ, for which there can be no substitute, constructed for the apprehension of truth."[8] With these arguments, backed by incontrovertible evidence, Ortega defends his right to produce his own philosophy from a personal point of view and from the perspective of Spain. Ortega says, "I am myself and my circumstance, and if I do not save it, I cannot save myself."[9] "My natural exit toward the universe is through the mountain passes of the Guadarrama or the plan of Ontígola. This sector of circumstantial reality forms the other half of my person; only through it can I integrate myself and be fully myself. The most recent biological science studies the living organism as a unit composed of the body and its particular environment...."[10] "Having exercised our eyes in gazing at the world map, let us now concentrate on the Guadarrama. Perhaps we shall find nothing profound, but we may be sure that the defect and the sterility derive from our glance. There is also a *logos* of the Manzanares River: this very humble stream, this liquid irony which laps the foundations of our capital, undoubtedly bears a drop of spirituality among its few drops of water."[11] In these quotations we find Ortega's philosophical position eloquently expressed.

True philosophy for Ortega is only that which is obtained by the practice of "vital reason," the organ of knowledge which is always individual and is only possessed by those who dare to think about the world for themselves, as it appears from a particular location. Abstract reason is a pure fiction that separates us from reality. "The abstract point of view yields only abstractions." It is impossible to give in such a short space a full idea of the richness of Ortega's thought, found in a widely varied body of work, composed of books with suggestive titles, such as *El Espectador, The Modern Theme, The Dehumanization of Art, The Revolt of the Masses*, etc., etc. In all of them, Ortega ponders the most troubling questions and problems that face the world today and that are part of its existence.

---

8. Ortega y Gasset, *The Modern Theme*, 91.
9. Ortega y Gasset, *Meditations*, 45.
10. Ortega y Gasset, *Meditations*, 45.
11. Ortega y Gasset, *Meditations*, 46.

By 1922, Ortega founded the *Revista de Occidente* and then a publishing house that produced a collection of chosen books that represent the best of European thought in our century. That is how a great number of Hispano-American readers came to know the names of Spengler, Scheler, Husserl, and many other great contemporary German philosophers. A valuable resource for students, the *Revista de Occidente*, which disappeared at the beginning of the Spanish Civil War, put within reach of American readers a series of books that are indispensable for acquiring philosophical culture. Ortega's editorial labor may have changed the direction of American thought and is one of the most important spiritual influences for which we are indebted to the great Spanish thinker.

But the most valuable lesson that Ortega imparts to the Hispanic American is the profoundly Spanish character of his thought and style. In them, we see a model approach that provides the philosophical foundations that legitimize the desire to attain a national philosophy.

The Preoccupation with Death[1]

The insistence with which the topic of death is presented across the panorama of contemporary culture is surprising, as if the majority of people who are otherwise working in very different intellectual fields could agree on this much. The preoccupation with death seems to consume every corner of our minds today with the intensity of an obsession, demanding us to confront the deepest mystery of existence. True, the thought of death has accompanied humankind from the moment we began to walk the earth, but, as some have observed, historically the problem of death has never plagued humankind so persistently. Pablo Landsberg claims that thinking about death is the rule, not the exception, during individualistic periods in which singular personalities flourish.[2] When someone dissolves into a group and lacks individuality, their death does not belong to them, in the same way their life doesn't; also, they might lack the consciousness of death because they do not consider it a permanent fact. The death of an individual member of a clan is as insignificant as a cell's death in tissue, which is repaired by substituting one cell for the other. When Greece's evolution came to an end and the *Polis* dissolved, a new degree of individuality appeared and, along with it, a new anxiety about death.

A similar phenomenon surfaced in the Renaissance and Reformation, when the medieval community was fully disintegrated. This period stands out for its abundance of outstanding personalities, and during this period the preoccupation with death was exacerbated.

The obsessive preoccupation with death, however, doesn't seem to be a symptom of calamitous times, such as ours, in which humanity

---

1. Published in *Letras de México* 2, no. 10, October 15, 1939.
2. Paul-Louis Landsberg was a student of Husserl, Heidegger, and Scheler. In this essay, Ramos is referring to his *Experience of Death*, and though he does not directly refer to them, he was likely also familiar with his *Introduction to Philosophical Anthropology* (1934) and *The Conception of a Person* (1934).

suffers all manner of catastrophes. If that were the case, the obsession with death would be constant throughout history, for there has never been a lack of wars, plagues, and hunger. Even in the best of times, people inevitably die. For this reason, we can't attribute the contemporary preoccupation with death exclusively to the impression left by the Great War and subsequent wars. On the contrary, facing the theatre of war, humanity tried to protect itself from anxiety and instinctively distracted itself in order to free itself from it. As for the combatants themselves, death was so familiar that they were desensitized and no longer found anything extraordinary or strange in it. For them, death ceased to be a problem.

We must admit, then, that our epoch has given rise to a new type of individuality for whom, because of individualization itself, the theme of death is salient. Someone will object that death has always been the subject of literature, philosophy, science, art, etc., so its presence in contemporary works is nothing new. Even so, one can point to a difference in how the theme is dealt with today, as opposed to in the past. Whereas before it is almost always scattered among other themes of greater and lesser importance, today it is frequently discussed on its own, a question that highlights an independent value. However, what's new is not just that the theme is treated on its own, but, more than anything, our attitude toward it and the concept of death itself as it is expressed in contemporary thought.

I mentioned the insistence with which the topic of death appears in contemporary philosophy, science, and literature. The name of Freud comes to mind: in his final works of psychology, he discusses a death instinct, which is like a nostalgia life has for inorganic existence. Heidegger's phenomenological analysis of "being and time," now famous, is perhaps the most profound reflection on the metaphysics of death recently produced. This problem is today linked to a school of thought that has been called "existential philosophy." Max Scheler has written an essay called "Death and Resurrection"; Pablo Landsberg, a small book titled "Experience of Death." Every day there appear literary works on the same theme. To cite just a few Mexican poets who were no doubt obsessed by death, recall "Death of the Blue Sky" by Ortiz de Montellano," "Nostalgia of Death" by Xavier Villaurrutia, and José Gorostiza's "Endless Death."

It is worth noting that classical philosophy and religion since the Middle Ages have only ignored the reality of death, have only denied the essence of death. For Plato, death represents the happy moment when the soul is liberated from the prison of the body, so that death only partially exists, only as access to a higher life. With some differences, religion in the Middle Ages adopted the same idea, and death was considered a veritable passage [*transito*][3] between two lives, one here on Earth and the other in heaven. At the end of the Classical Age, Epicureans and Stoics addressed the problem at length, regarding the fear of death as one of the torments that embitters life. To cure themselves of this fear, they devised what Landsberg accurately called the sophism of the nonexistence of death. Epicurus said that we should not fear death because life and death never meet, which amounts to saying that we should not be concerned with death. As long as we exist, death is not present; and once it comes, we no longer exist.[4] When Lucretius expanded on this idea, he discovered its true meaning. No part of the sensibility remains to suffer and mourn the death of another. Sensation and consciousness are completely annihilated. We lack the space here to quote the many opinions that affirm this view of the essence of death, but for our purposes those that I have transcribed, which are the most significant, suffice. However, I cannot resist quoting one paragraph of [Manuel García] Morente, who articulates the Spanish Christian view of death in clear terms: "The conceptions that human beings have formed of death can be reduced to two: those for whom death is a conclusion or end, and those for whom death is a starting point or beginning."[5] There are those who consider death the termination of life. For them, life

---

3. This definition survives. One translation of the word *transito* is "the passage of death."

4. Epicurus, "Letter to Menoeceus," in *Principal Doctrines*, trans. Russel Geer (Library of Liberal Arts, 1978), 54.

5. This appears in an essay titled, "Simbolización del estilo español: El Caballero Cristiano," in which Morente describes the Spanish way or style of being.

consists of this life, that which they are currently living and of which they have an immediate intuition, rich and unmistaken.

Others, by contrast, see death as a beginning, the initiation of a life more truly lived, eternal life. Death, for them, does not bring to a close, but opens. It is affirmation, not negation, and it is the moment they start to realize all their hopes. But what are the consequences of this conception of death? For one thing, a matching and corresponding conception of life. Because it is clear that when death is considered a conclusion and end, life must be something supremely worthwhile, the most worthwhile, and the highest value among countless other values. By contrast, when death is considered the beginning of eternal life, true life, earthy existence—the life that death cancels—must be a mere passage or step toward, or transitory preparation for, essential and eternal life. This life, then, will be of secondary, subordinate, conditional, inferior value. Is this not the greatest paradox of them all, that which makes life of death and death of life?

Letter to W. W. Norton & Company, Inc.
T. B. Irving

September 1st, 1941

W. W. Norton & Company, Inc.
70 Fifth avenue
New York City.

Dear Sirs:
    During the past two summers, I have had a good chance to get to know the intellectual leaders of Mexico, and while talking recently with Dr. Alfonso Reyes, the head of the Colegio de México, he told me how badly he felt that there was so little opportunity for Mexican thought to reach the United States, and wished there could be some means of translating some of the recent works, especially those that the Colegio de México has put out.

    I don't know if you have heard of this institution, but it was founded by former President Cárdenas on the model of the Collège de France, and it promises to be one of the most important centers of American culture in the future. At least, this is my opinion from the people I have met who are connected with it, their program for the improvement of Mexican scientific and academic life through the foundation of laboratories and chairs, and especially by the imposing list of publications they have managed to put out in a relatively short time, including works of native Mexicans and Spaniards resident in México (I can send you a copy of their catalogue if you are curious about the matter).

    However, Dr. Reyes and I talked of those that would be of most interest in English translation, like Justo Sierra's <u>Evolución política del pueblo mexicano</u>, but decided that for a start the best to work on would be "Hacia un nuevo humanismo" ("Toward a New Humanism") by Prof. Samuel Ramos, one of Mexico's younger and more promising thinkers. As a result, I promised Dr. Reyes that I would take the matter up when I returned to this country, and immediately thought of you as possible publishers, both because of the type of books you publish and also because Prof. Ramos's Humanismo (which came out last year) is supposed to have elicited much praise on the part of José Ortega y Gasset and to have been used by him in his recent lectures.

The book has several advantages: first of all its intrinsic value—while I dare not say the work is monumental, yet I do not believe you would ever be sorry to have introduced a significant contemporary to the United States reading public; secondly, the book is timely, in some ways as timely as Croce's History as the story of liberty; and above all, as it contains only 154 pages in the Spanish edition, it would make a rather popular small bound volume selling for from $1.75 to $2.00 (the price is 3 pesos in the paper-jacket edition now).

As for contents, the book is an attempt to restate what the author considers a vital problem to-day, which is best summed up in the full title: "Toward a new humanism; a program for a philosophy philosophical anthropology."

Prof. Ramos starts in the first chapter by stating the crisis that humanity faces, that the philosopher, despairing of solving the problems of the real world, has sought refuge in idealism, and as a result the man of action tries to solve the same problems by purely pragmatic methods. This has led to dualism and a confusion expressed in the divorce between our theory and our action. Therefore we have lost our sense of the true values of life and find ourselves perplexed by the bifurcation between duty and necessity. It is up to philosophy to reorient itself toward a solution of this dilemma.

"Philosophy exists in connection with certain problems of a general character that neither religion nor any particular branch of science is called upon to solve, but that fall to a discipline which tries to grasp reality as a whole and according to a higher plan. At the outset, philosophy is the consciousness of these problems, and its duty is defining and stating them. . . . This book should be considered a sincere effort to assimilate those philosophical currents having the greatest weight in present-day thought (pp. 31–32)."[1]

Prof. Ramos then proceeds to organize the most important thoughts of the day, like Nicolai Hartmann, Bergson, Ortega, and Max Scheler, and the[n] asserts that his personal solution is that man must form a more scientific and at the same time philosophic concept of humanity, utilizing for this view the fruits of modern anthropological investigation. The first point is Descartes's key principle: man's consciousness of his own existence. From there, man comes to realize that he is not a creature that IS, but one that is becoming (something of Spengler and of Bergson here), and above all, something that can be different. In other words, man knows he can influence his own destiny, and his chief preoccupation is what he "must be." "Human life is an incessant tendency toward objectives of value.... Culture, as Scheler has well seen it, is only a process of humanization radiating from man and extending into the nature surrounding him. (p. 67)."

What is man's mission in the midst of this process?

"The Greeks, in theory, raised nature to man's level, while the moderns have lowered man to nature's. (p. 68)" The New Humanism would try to see that man reached his full capacity. "The problem of anthropology is rather to determine how those particular elements come together as a whole, what relations there are between them and what is the essential structure that they form. It ascertains if these elements can be ordered in a hierarchy conforming to any objective scale of values. (p. 72)."

Prof. Ramos lays great stock in a theory of values. "The aim of culture is to awaken the fullest possible consciousness of values, and not as is wrongly supposed, merely to accumulate knowledge. (p. 93) Values are not, then, inert like Platonic ideas; a dynamic principle drives them beyond the ideal plans on which they find themselves to a plane of real facts. (p. 94) What we call civilization and culture is precisely that transformation of nature, which orients it so that man may realize certain ends which he lays down.... As a whole,

---

[1]. The pagination throughout this letter is in the original and refers to the first edition of the Spanish text.

civilization and culture mean a labor tending to raise nature to the level where it acquires sense and value. (p. 96)"

But beyond this there are moral values, and by these Ramos does not imply those "forms of conduct having the external appearance of morality but which at bottom obey Prejudices, impulses, social mimetisms, etc. (p. 102)" It is rather that man is free, and morality is a guide as to where this freedom should lead. The reason there appears to be a problem between free will and predestination is that everything man does is conditioned by the material conditions of his past and present, but that does not preclude action in the future.

This brings into the discussion the distinction between the person and the individual: the individual is the inert unit of society, while the person is the unit that can and does exert an influence upon the mass. "Personality awakens the individual's mastery and control over the acts of his life; it belongs to the man who does not let himself be dragged by his inclinations or the circumstances surrounding him, but who imposes himself on everything and dictates a life of conduct and a stamp of his own on his activity. (p. 127) If personality originates in the individual ego, its direction is nonetheless essentially centrifugal. In man there are impulses leading exclusively to the affirmation of individuality, but they are centripetal movements. (p. 128)" Personalities are not formed however by selfish domination of others, but by "forgetting and giving themselves up, in order to realize ends and values that are purely objective and impersonal. (p. 138)"

What marks one individual from another and gives him personality? "In the tastes of each individual, in his likes, in his dislikes, he constantly displays the same way of preferring and rejecting. (pp. 129–30)" These mannerisms are his psychic sense of values, and from them springs his character. Prof. Ramos concludes that there is an interaction between his character and personality, and that "character is the raw material of personality and also the limit that marks the range of its possibilities. (p. 130)" It is a spiritual aspect of life, and hence "those men fit to be great personalities must assume great responsibilities before history. Their nonconformity to current values predestines them to be creators of new values. Once these are objectified in works of culture they become permanent part of the public domain and are vulgarized. Then there will be other spirits fleeing from vulgarity who will find new values, which will be popularized in their turn, and on and on endlessly. (p. 135)."

There are also collective personalities, such as groups and nations, who serve as even more important propagators of culture, and through which individual personalities may reach the world in general. But they too can become dead and inert, and it is the phenomenon we see to-day when men feel that "civilization, contradicting its original destiny, instead of favoring life, is converting it into an instrument of death. And thus man reaches the paradoxical situation of having to defend himself from his own civilization. (p. 143)"

This is the present-day problem. "Fortunately, part of mankind has saved its clear consciousness, and is on guard against the danger, preparing to defend man's most precious values with all its energy. (p. 144)" If it seems otherwise, it is only that "material conditions influence culture in a negative fashion (p. 147)" and it is up to man to realize this fact and take his destiny back into his own hands. "Man and no one else is responsible for his history. (p. 145)"

I hope I have been able to give you a fair idea of this work. If the review offered in this letter fails to impress you, it will be rather my fault than Mr. Ramos's. And if the subject is too short, the author has another small book, El perfil del hombre y de la cultura en México ("The Profile of Man and Culture in Mexico") in which he applies his "philosophical anthropology" to the study of the Mexican people. This could be added to form a regular-sized work that would offer your readers direct application as well as theory of his philosophy.

If you want to see the book Hacia un nuevo humanismo itself, you can either drop me a line and I will send you a copy, or you can write to

        Dr. Alfonso Reyes
        Colegio de México,
        Pánuco 63,
        México, D. F., México.

Thank you in any case for your attention, and I shall be very glad to cooperate with you in preparing a competent translation. Despite all the recent display of friendship on the part of this country for things south of the Río Grande, Latin America has really had surprisingly little chance to speak for itself. As Europe becomes more separate from us through exhaustion or pessimism, we may be glad to draw on a vigorous and growing culture, and I believe this offers your house the opportunity to be in the van of such a movement.

Very truly you[r]s,
T. B. Irving.

The "Toward" of Samuel Ramos
José Gaos[1]

The publication of Samuel Ramos's most recent book, *Toward a New Humanism*,[2] can be called without qualification a major event. It encompasses everything I hope to at least touch upon in this review.

Contemporary philosophy, that which—among all that professes to be philosophy in the contemporary period—is endowed with validity and immediate potential, can be traced back precisely to 1900, the year Husserl's *Logical Investigations* was published.[3] From our vantage point, phenomenology and its offshoots appear to be the dominant philosophy of the first half of this century. In the first phase of phenomenology, its idealism reinforced the idealism of the prevailing neo-Kantian philosophy, mainly that of the Marburg school. But soon, the two currents, neo-Kantianism and phenomenology, were steered resolutely toward realism: Külpe and Scheler, respectively, represent this new direction best. Nicolai Hartmann's *Fundamentals of the Metaphysics of Cognition* provides an important synthesis of phenomenology and the neo-Kantianism of the Marburg School, as they moved gradually from idealism to realism, and, as a synthesis, it

---

1. Published in *Letras de México* 2, no. 20: 1–2, 8.
2. Published by La Casa de España en México.
3. The phrase in Spanish is *la filosofía actual*, which translates literally to "present philosophy" or "philosophy today," but which can also be translated as "modern philosophy" or "contemporary philosophy." I have chosen "contemporary philosophy" because Gaos is discussing a movement of philosophy that he traces back to 1900, and which is significant in part for standing opposed to "modern philosophy," understood as the European tradition of philosophy between 1650–1900, that is, the philosophy that stretches back to Descartes and is defined by the problem of representation. If one were to opt for "modern philosophy," it would be "modern" in the sense that Ortega has in mind in his book, *The Modern Theme*, but there again, "modern" is closer to "contemporary," and its contrast is modern European philosophy. In writing *la filosofía actual*, Gaos is more or less referring to "the philosophy of life."

represents a milestone on the path of contemporary philosophy. In addition, within neo-Kantianism emerged the philosophy of values of the Baden School, developed most fully by Rickert, and within phenomenology emerged the material ethics of Scheler, and a whole philosophy of values besides. Once again, it was Hartmann, in his *Ethics*, who offered a synthesis when he characterized Husserl's critique of psychologism in the first volume of the *Logical Investigations* as the initial impetus to restore the realism of the ideal, which is or amounts to part of that neo-Kantian and phenomenological realism and those philosophies of values. That is how a pluralist *Weltanschauung* was established and began to be taught widely, pluralist in the sense that it viewed the world as integrated by regions of objects: physical, psychological, ideal, metaphysical, values. But this appealing view didn't last long, at least not in philosophy, even though old ideas tend to linger in the classroom. One region triumphed and dominated the rest to the point of threatening the autonomy of other regions that seemed to have established their independence. In many corners of contemporary philosophy, a philosophy of the person pulsated or was even occasionally jotted down—a natural consequence of returning to the psychic, to its irreducible singularity, espoused in no uncertain terms by Husserl's teacher, Brentano, since 1874.[4] Among the rest of his philosophies, Scheler's philosophy of spirit, part of his philosophy of values, culminated in a philosophy of the person. But the abundant vitality of this great agonist of thought, protean like that of the mythical hero, drove the spirit unflinchingly toward the sociology of knowledge—in which reason, the classical, permanent feature of human nature, is historicized to a certain extent—which is but support for a *cosmotheology* of the Urge [*impulso*] and the Spirit.[5] In this philosophical context, Heidegger's *Being and Time* appeared in 1926, and so began the tide of "existential philosophy," leading to

---

4. This is likely a reference to Brentano's *Psychology from an Empirical Standpoint*, published in 1874, especially since it is about Hartmann's *Philosophy of the Unconscious*, and considered essential in laying the foundations of phenomenology.

5. In *Max Scheler: A Concise Introduction to the World of a Great Thinker*, Manfred Frings argues that *Drang* (Spanish *impulso*) is better translated as "urge," not "drive."

the situation of, in, through, without, above, and behind the ocean that existentialism is today. How will I translate *Dasein*, what we call life, as when we say, "such is life"? Not literally. However, rendered faithfully and with the fewest misleading connotations than perhaps any other possible translation, it is the entity characterized by a certain ontic and ontological primordiality. Heidegger retroactively cast light on and put the emphasis on the historicism—latent in the penumbra of the past—of one of Sprangers's students, Dilthey, moving closer to the philosophies of value and of the person, particularly Scheler's. Likewise, Heidegger modified the relief map of Bergson's philosophy: his naturalism is buried under ancient shade, and his pre-existentialist themes are lifted to dazzling timeliness. In Spain, at least as early as his *Meditations on Quixote*, Ortega transitioned from the idealism of his teachers in Marburg to the realism of "vital reason," in which we find one of the original philosophies of life, original in its motivation, its particular content, and in much of its development, even though it agrees with the others in the rest of its development, a natural consequence given the community surrounding its historical origin and general orientation.

Ramos's book divides contemporary philosophy, which I have presented historically, into topics. Its point of departure is an affirmation of realism, which does not object to the priority of the problem and theory of knowledge granted by not-so-contemporary philosophy: "that" need to ensure before all else the reality of all that follows from it, reality that more recent philosophy *gives* us with more certainty than can be gained from any possible *search* for it. But Ramos does not turn a blind eye to the latest philosophy (see the section "The Ontological Foundation of Knowledge"). He simply doesn't draw out all the consequences relevant to the composition of the book. The reason for his indifference lies in what for me is the nature of the book, that which explains all of its peculiarities, but I will come back to this presently.

Alongside the realism with which he begins, Ramos juxtaposes the historicity of reason in the form of "the variation of categories." Reality, as it's known through the variable categories of reason, is presented early under a pluralist *Weltanschauung* as a reality divided into regions of objects. Privileged among these regions is human existence, "which is the most independent of them all and through which the others intersect." On this point, Boutroux and Bergson are given credit as the predecessors to existential philosophy. It is a fitting debt of gratitude paid by Ramos to French philosophy, to which he very much owes—in every sense—part of his development, and it is vindication in itself, which the latest philosophy has not entirely stopped acknowledging.

In the "Agenda for a Philosophical Anthropology," outlined by Ramos, defining the essence of the human being is presented as the first stage of the discipline, understood in accordance with Husserl's phenomenological method or Heidegger's phenomenology of human existence. Husserl's phenomenology is included only for its method of describing essences. "Among the ideas concerning the human, we have to pick out a basic set of ideas supported by the strongest evidence in order to determine the axioms of anthropology." Heidegger's analysis of *Dasein* is found in "Axioms of Human Ontology," though this section is not simply a summary of Heidegger. On the contrary, what is taken from Heidegger's analytic is relatively minimal. One extremely important point in the book, truly central, is that "the ontology of human existence cannot ignore the fact that humans are 'political animals,' beings who live in society," and it recognizes, "alluding to another important fact of human existence," that "the human is a moral being, that is, a being that faces demands and duties of an ideal nature. Human consciousness is not only consciousness of what is, but also of what 'ought to be,' which is like a bridge that leads humans from the world of facts to the world of values." The substance of the second half of the book, the philosophy of values and of the person, is introduced at this point in the sections on philosophical anthropology and the ontology of human existence. The rest of the agenda for philosophical anthropology consists of a brief overview of Scheler's typology of the conceptions of the human being, provided in order to trace the arc of humanism in history; of a new appraisal, positive and limited, of instincts, largely Ramos's own; and of a study of the layers of the human being, based on Ortega y Gasset's distinction between vitality, soul, and spirit. When they are inserted into the ontology of human existence in the manner described above, the philosophy of values and of the person fit neatly into the structure of the book, except for very minor incongruencies that aren't essential to its development. Ramos mainly follows, as he was obliged to do, the great innovators, Scheler and Hartmann, in a sequence of their theories, brought together in a sort of synthesis through the dependence of the latter on the former, but he does not question the differences and discrepancies between them, which are not few and far between, even on major points. But this leads us to considerations that should be treated separately.

The content of the book gives it the character of a breviary of contemporary philosophy, as my summary of it suggests. As a breviary, critics and professors alike will no doubt recommend it—I now include myself among this group—and it will be used by both students and the layperson. And its character and style, sober and clear, promises that it will be successful. However, the book is not expressly intended to teach, even though the author is a professor by trade. It is not written exactly according to a didactic plan, nor is it organized in the way a textbook would be. If it is widely used to teach, such success would be incidental to its aim. Instead, the aim and composition of the book reflect a set of motives and articulations that are more profound than merely didactic exercises.

Ramos's way of summarizing contemporary philosophy, which I've surveyed historically, does not present the philosophemes of contemporary philosophy in chronological order; instead, the themes are arranged according to the internal theoretical relations among them. In the end, then, we can unambiguously affirm that Ramos provides a systemization of the history of contemporary philosophy, or, what amounts to the same, a system of the history of contemporary philosophy, even though the author modestly claims that "the aim of these chapters is not to produce a philosophical treatise that presents its problems systematically. They should be read only as a selection of philosophical ideas arranged according to a personal perspective." Readers and critics have the right to read a book, not how the author says they should, but as it is, and with the above summary of the history of contemporary philosophy and the content of the book, I hope to have shown what Ramos's book actually is.

Now, at the very least, a system like Ramos's ought to lay out problems for those willing to tackle them, especially for those who are aware of the function and meaning of a philosophical problem, as Ramos claims to be. The first such problem is that of choosing what to include, which is a problem of critique and evaluation, resolved according to the idea one has of philosophical truth in relation to the history of philosophy. Not every contemporary philosophy will enter, can enter, into the system, and of those that do, not all enter to the same degree. In Ramos's system, Scheler is clearly the dominant figure, and there is much more Hartmann than Heidegger and Husserl, even though many believe Heidegger and Husserl represent something more current in philosophy—for being truer, naturally—than Scheler and especially Hartmann. Then there are problems of formulation. How does one form a system of different philosophies that attribute their respective authenticity to their mutual distinction? To cite just one example of this kind of serious problem for Ramos: Heidegger's analysis of Dasein is presented as part of philosophical anthropology, even though Heidegger dedicates an entire paragraph of *Being in Time* to distinguishing it from anthropology, psychology, and biology. Finally, there is the fundamental problem of the venture itself. The classical problem—Aristotle and Hegel's problem—is the formidable task of reconstructing the history of philosophy in the form of a system. This is the general problem of systematizing history. The history of philosophies has to be written philosophically to make possible a philosophy that organizes the history of philosophies....[6] Ramos's book does not explicitly raise these questions. However, his selection is not thereby less justified, nor is its unifying thread any less rigorous than is normal for a book of its kind. And, concerning the problem of the system of history, it is true that this book offers the solution of repeated attempts of organizing a system historically. But it is no less true that if this book had raised and discussed these questions, it would have gained a new, third dimension, one of profundity, density, and dramatic interest. However, that would have been a

---

6. The ellipses throughout this review are in the original.

different book than the one Ramos set out to write, and he is justified for not having done so.

Ramos did not want to get stuck or tangled up in problems. He went straight to offering a synthesis, to creation and recreation. He himself describes his book as "a summary of the author's philosophical convictions." A book of convictions—not a book of problems! But can it be that the convictions of someone whose originality is so principled, so uncompromising, someone so profoundly Mexican and temperamentally unique, someone such as Samuel Ramos, are the ideas of Hartmann and Scheler? For my own part, that's not how I see it. As far as I'm concerned, a thinker's philosophical convictions are formed mostly in the beginning, in response to a catalyst. They are never actually made up by the foreign ideas one adopts, but by the reasons for which one adopts them, reasons that can't be taken from someone else, personal reasons that, if one is first drawn to them unconsciously or barely conscious, once they are developed and consciously expressed in the form of reasons, they become the thinker's original and individual philosophy. And this is how I understand the case of Ramos. His breviary of contemporary philosophy, this summary of the author's philosophical convictions, manifestly has the appearance of a text born of "a kind of self-examination, a liquidation of ideas," as the author himself describes its origin. For Ramos, this book is a settling of scores with contemporary philosophy, in order to . . .

Ramos's systematization of the history of contemporary philosophy is bookended by a first chapter on "the crisis of humanism" and a "conclusion" that returns to the theme of the opening chapter. Inherent in the human being is a duality of spirit and matter. Traditionally, a certain philosophical idea, and culture more generally, exalted the former by devaluing the latter. The result was a revolt of the material, which includes the aspects and circumstances that constitute or are symptomatic of our crisis today, the present day. It is a crisis grounded, then, in the very idea of the human being. In this section of Ramos's book, the problem and its root are laid out. The problematicity of philosophy itself is undeniably critical in a book of philosophy. Is philosophy a force for good, as it has traditionally considered itself and been so judged by others? Is it a force at all, something that historical materialism calls into question, and that is even called into question by Scheler and Hartmann's claim that the Spirit is impotent? At the very bottom of our crisis today lies this crisis of the power of spirit, of ideas, of reason . . .

This section constitutes the authentic part of the book. It is here in the first and concluding chapters that we find in *Toward a New Humanism* the philosophy of the author of the *Profile of Man and Culture in Mexico*. The spirit of the author of the *Profile* can also be delineated in the characteristic pondering of the new humanism that proposes, that advocates: "Whose direction is upward from below," since it must raise human values once again to their proper place, values that the revolt of the material has lowered below their proper place, and it must do so for the sake of "the synthesis of antagonistic forces" in the human being and "the reestablishment of harmony, first in one's individual being and then in their historical existence." And the deepest conviction driving the proposal of this new humanism, and the struggle for it, is a conviction on which the death or survival of philosophy hinges: a conviction in the power of reason, of ideas, of the spirit: the conviction of its own power. Despite all the Schelerian and Hartmannian philosophemes absorbed, it says: authenticity within is inalienable but bursts forth. For example: "It is important to acknowledge that contemporary philosophy has examined this global crisis tirelessly and has successfully revealed different paths toward salvation." Salvation through philosophy . . .

Settling scores with modern philosophy, in order to . . . move onto, definitively, without getting tangled up in previous questions, one's own philosophy. For that reason, "toward" seems to me the most important word in the title, and that's why I have given this article a title that the reader may have found surprising. The event that is Ramos's book consists, in sum, in the decisive role it plays in helping to achieve the assimilation of contemporary philosophy for Mexico. Known more or less directly and authentically, more or less widespread and discussed, there is no longer anything essential in contemporary philosophy that is unknown to Mexican thought. Moreover, Mexican thought is at a critical juncture and must not get in the way of its *own* thinking—beginning with positing and resolving the problem of whether the "ownness" of Mexican thought will admit philosophical ownness as a part of it, or, if not so much, merely determinate forms of contemporary and foreign philosophy.[7] As for this text, situated as it is in between two well-established generations and younger Mexican teachers, and given the combination of the maturity of its life and the pause in philosophy abroad caused by the culmination of the crisis in the form of war, and having returned to his own theme, that of the profile of man and culture in his country, nobody seems more "condemned by God" than Samuel Ramos.

---

7. This passage is particularly difficult to render in English. However, the thought behind it seems central to the thesis of the article and to Gaos's interest in Mexican philosophy more broadly, so it is worth examining further. In the original, Gaos writes: "Más o menos directa y auténticamente conocida, más o menos difundida y compartida, la filosofía actual ya no tiene nada esencial ignorado del pensamiento mexicano. Por lo tanto, éste se halla en el trance y en el deber de superarse hacia un pensamiento de sí propio—empezando por plantearse y resolver el problema de si la 'propiedad' de este pensamiento admitirá como forma de él la filosófica, o, si no tanto, determinadas formas meramente modernas y extranjeras de la filosofía." As I understand it, Gaos here is provoking Mexican philosophers by asking, now that they are aware of contemporary philosophy, whether Mexican *philosophy* will participate in the larger project of Mexican *thought*, that is, whether it will attempt to be authentically its *own*, characterized by a kind of "ownness," or whether it will merely take on the form of modern, European philosophy. It is the difference between *assimilating* European philosophy, as Gaos suggests in the previous sentence, and *imitating* it. This is the very same project, and provocation, that Ramos introduces in his *Profile of Man and Culture in Mexico*.

"Toward a New Humanism"
Eduardo Nicol[1]

The Casa de España en México recently published a new book with the above title by Professor Samuel Ramos. The book offers a valuable overview of the basic problems facing humanity today, and of the pivotal steps contemporary philosophy is taking in response to them. But a thinker of Samuel Ramos's sensibility cannot keep to a purely didactic style of exposition; and even when he achieves a clarity that makes challenging theories and questions accessible to anyone, the very same clarity indicates how much they have matured in Ramos's philosophy. Only when a problem has been internalized and authentically made one's own is it possible to make sense of it, disentangling the root of the problem from the confusion that surrounds it when it assails one from without. In this way, Samuel Ramos is like a protagonist of the ideas that he expounds; his personality is present not only in the position he takes toward them, but even in the spirit governing the logical task of systematically organizing and articulating its themes. Concerning the scope and object of his text, Ramos exhibits the confident self-awareness of a *maestro*: "The ideas presented in this book are a summary of the author's philosophical convictions. The exposition was born from a kind of self-examination, a liquidation of ideas, undertaken in order to participate in a philosophical debate taking place in the contemporary world." Nevertheless, this debate has deep implications for the existence of man and culture, and Ramos lends the present situation a dramatic quality. "Civilization, such as it is organized, seems like a diabolic plan to leave humans without souls." Elsewhere: "Salvation depends not only on a change

---

1. Although this review was published in 1941, this translation was based on the version found in *Nuestro Samuel Ramos: Homenaje*, edited by Adela Palacios, published in Mexico in 1960.

in material conditions, but also, at the same time, on rebuilding our spiritual world."

Because in fact the spiritual world of the modern human being has collapsed. But the real catastrophe is not what we are currently witnessing in the Western world. Even when the dissolution of traditional political forms—brought to crisis through war—effectively makes spiritual life impossible for the affected regions, the problem would not be as serious as it is if it were not an indication and consequence of more profound evils of a more distant origin. The crisis, in effect, is so complex and large that it affects all phenomena of life and every region of culture. And since every region can legitimately speak of itself as being in crisis, then, even though each perspective is partial, each region from which that perspective is projected is not independent, but interdependent and connected to the rest: crisis of religiosity, crisis of morality, crisis in the principles of science, crisis in the law, economic crisis, crisis in how human beings coexist.

The mission of the philosopher has always been to reduce the confused diversity of phenomena to a unity. Well, the unity that explains the mass confusion of the present day resides in the human being. It is the human who is confused. When every form, institution, and tradition of culture falls into crisis, it is because the human being, who creates and nourishes them and who is nourished by them and lives in them, has fallen into crisis. Today we are witnessing—we are actors in—the discordance between our way of seeing and the products that others create for our comfort in the world. When this discordance doesn't exist—it didn't exist a century ago—the path of life is level and straight. Today life is not possible, but given that we nevertheless continue to live, the blatant contradiction between both experiences makes life problematic. Life seems strange to us. Today the human being longs for life—as opposed to living[2]—they long

---

2. "El hombre hoy se extraña de la vida—en vez de vivirla, sin más." The contrast here is between living and having something to live for, as in the song, "Ya no vivo por vivir" ["I no longer live (just) to live"]. This distinction is a constant theme in Ramos's writings and is the basis of his understanding of wisdom. In "Twenty Years of Education in Mexico (1941)," for instance, Ramos writes: "In my judgment, Vasconcelos was the first to understand this very simple truth (so simple

for, or are a stranger to, themselves. In other words, humans have become a problem to themselves. This is the fundamental problem, the most sweeping and basic.

How did we get here? The human being has always had some ideas concerning what it means to be human—almost always favorable. Be it a creature of God, or a rational being, when humans have reflected on nature, they always return to the image of a being sovereign over the world, with legislative and executive power over it. Medieval philosophy succeeded in marrying these two ideas (one of Judeo-Cristian origin and the other of Greek origin), which may in the end be irreconcilable. At any rate, the aspiration of rationalism, the faith in the indefinite progress of our rational control of the world, has led to the divorce between the two: it has undermined religious faith without successfully replacing it with a comparably robust principle. For its own part, science has also failed in its attempt to provide an organizing and guiding principle of human existence. This is still worth proclaiming somewhat forcefully because the human being now does not know where to look for it.

Science cannot serve as a guide for human life—that is, of human consciousness—because (the same goes for all philosophy that begins with a theory of knowledge) it trades vital experience, which is unified in all its complexity, for a dualism that thinks only in terms of the subject and object. As Scheler says, a complete theory of knowledge involves a manner of being, a life, a test or attempt. The primary thing is the close interaction with things. All criteria are subsequent and artificial. Positivism and idealism are both guilty of this; they both make the same mistake. The object loses its peculiar quality of being in dialogue with the human being; it stops being a living object, and the human becomes an object. And whatever life there is in the human, that which is distinctive and irreducible, is carefully put aside.

---

that nobody had seen it): that what most urgently has to be taught to the Mexican people is how to live. Because although it seems that knowing how to live is a question of instinct, what is certain is that all peoples require long and painful experience to learn the science of life. There we find our people, who know how to *endure* life, which is not the same as knowing how to *live*, but rather, knowing how to die, which is the negation of all wisdom" (56).

The vital is given a biological interpretation, failing to realize that humans live out their animal lives differently from other animals, since it is the only animal that lives *with* its body.

Once the human is considered a natural being, they are decomposed like any other object, and, thus depersonalized, they enter the sphere of abstraction where science operates and where nothing has value or meaning. All of reality evaporates into a game of relations that are ultimately grounded in the relation of identity. The sciences, the model of mathematics above all, create a system of signs that constitutes a [value]-neutral representation of reality to which all logical thought adheres, and from which enthusiasm, anxiety, and all desire are excluded. The communicability of scientific truth has been considered a success, thanks to the standards of pragmatism. Science was believed to be a reliable path because it was useful in our attempt to control nature. This is how science developed into technology; and insofar as the human has been dehumanized, science has shifted from having a theoretical use for reason to having a pragmatic, utilitarian use. Truth is no longer the alignment of thought with reality, but the domination of reality by means of thought. It becomes one more instrument of domination. Propaganda is substituted for personal reflection. And the millstone is substituted for ideas and feelings in the communion of human beings.

The path to salvation, then, consists in delivering the human from this new great sin that they have once again fallen into out of a thirst for power. They have to be brought back to their human condition, taking them out of the sphere of the neutral, the homogenous, the insignificant, the indifferent, or the interchangeable, that is, out of sphere of the physical. The human being does not live as the rock falls; the human lives with the rock, be it cliff or statue, differently from the way one rock is located next to another. The human is not an identical being, but a historical being. The condition and structure of their manner of being needs to be investigated, and, as Professor Ramos explains, the content of this investigation constitutes a science—anthropology, which, even though it can't share in common the principles, methods, or object of the natural sciences, we still call a science for want of a better term.

The Humanism of Samuel Ramos: A Guide for Contemporary Society
Rafael Moreno M.[1]

– I –

Ramos surged into the history of philosophy bearing the traits that would accompany him until his final days: at odds with his philosophical milieu, an assiduous reader of the most recent developments, preoccupied by national questions and by the destiny of humanity, a philosopher who preferred the essay over the systematic treatise.[2] His character and authorship are lessons that teach us how to philosophize, preserving a faith in the Mexican mind and in the defining features of *lo humano*.[3] He models two different ways of thinking about originality: to make universal culture one's own by means of re-creation, through the modest act of rethinking what has already been thought, and at the same time, to identify "a selection of philosophical ideas arranged according to a personal perspective" (both human existence and the destiny of humanity, the substance of civilization and culture, on the one hand; on the other, the history, modes of being, and the problems facing a concrete human being, the Mexican).[4] If in *The Profile of Man and Culture in Mexico*, published in 1934, philosophy

---

1. Published in *Excelsior: El Periódico de la Vida Nacional*, July 6, 1969.

2. See Martin S. Stabb, *In Quest of Identity: Patterns in the Spanish American Essay of Ideas, 1890–1960* (Chapel Hill: University of North Carolina Press, 1967).

3. I have left this phrase untranslated in order to draw the contrast between *lo humano* and *lo mexicano*.

4. Compare to what William Barrett says about originality: "What T. S. Eliot has said in the context of literature—that the genuinely original creation is that which draws most deeply upon tradition even when it shakes up and transforms this tradition—applies just as sure to science [and philosophy]. The whole body of science is a continuous stream from the beginnings of human consciousness, and the genuinely new scientific creation is the one that reaches most deeply

is applied to the nationality of culture, in *Hypothesis*, which appeared in 1928, aside from distancing himself against his teacher Antonio Caso, Ramos was already beginning to analyze existence and form his own opinions on contemporary philosophy.

– II –

Since then, the recurring theme that dominated Ramos's reading, reflections, classes, and conversations was the human being. Everything tended toward understanding and expressing what it means to be human. Even his essays on aesthetics and final studies on logical empiricism, rather than construct a systematic theory, had a way of capturing the human contribution. He arrived at humanity through the Mexican, and, at the same time, he elevated the human being from the Mexican. With both passion and objectivity, he examined our past and our historical stumbles, and he wrote a book that José Gaos called the first philosophy of Mexican history and culture; but the scope of the reflection transcends the national, since its boundary is human existence. The perspective he speaks about, which he inherited in equal measure from the tradition represented by Caso and Vasconcelos, and by Ortega y Gasset, reflects two forms of salvation: the salvation of the human being and the salvation of the Mexican. The instruments at his disposal were his knowledge of contemporary philosophy and his familiarity with our history and culture. Hence, the *Profile* and *Toward a New Humanism* are his two most important works. The 1934 text anticipates and introduces the one published in 1940, and the latter supplies the theory that transforms the former into a fully philosophical text. The *Profile*, employing contemporary philosophical and psychological tools, is a philosophical anthropology of the Mexican person; Ramos explicitly describes *Toward a New Humanism* as an agenda for a philosophical anthropology. The analysis of existence, then, of human existence, and the existence of a concrete human being. Neither work is brought to

---

into the body of this thought in order to give us some new direction." *Death of the Soul: From Descartes to the Computer* (Garden City: Anchor Books, 1986), 5.

a conclusion but instead provides a philosophical roadmap. In fact, today the various essays that constitute the *Profile* can be read as a final chapter of *Toward a New Humanism*, or conversely, *Toward a New Humanism* can be read as the theoretical culmination of Ramos's meditations on Mexico.

Both works address, in their own way, a single problem: the failure of the human being. Mexicans vacillate between imitation and self-abandonment, between undervaluing themselves and overvaluing the foreigner, between the reality of their own world and imported culture, between nationalism and Europeanism. Humans are being annihilated in a crisis that touches every aspect of existence, since they live according to a false way of valuing that garbles distinct planes and results in a confusion of ideas and values. While the national predicament is the result of an irrational history, of a superimposed culture, the contemporary crisis is the culmination of modern times.

The diagnosis follows similar lines: Mexicans don't participate in genuine culture; contemporary civilization compels them to distance themselves from truly human ends. But imitation, duality, and deception are not inherent in the Mexican, just as the confusion of values has only suppressed, but has not destroyed, the spiritual virtues where the authentic vocation of culture resides. *Toward a New Humanism* and the *Profile* suggest that the crisis will come to an end when we reacquaint ourselves with the values unique to human nature, that is, when Mexicans embrace and achieve the categories particular to them and when we return to the unity of being human. It is not for nothing that Ramos explicitly says in both books that he was inspired "by the eternal validity of the Socractic maxim: know thyself." More than once he says that the solution lies in an examination, in an awareness, of what it means to be human in one's regional particularity and what the human being essentially is *qua* human being. He concludes that the double crisis is more apparent than real when looked at from the ontological constitution of *lo humano*. For both Mexico and the world, the decline originates from a great historical error, which the philosopher must warn us against and correct.

– III –

These propositions make Ramos a modern philosopher. He raises the issue of our unique existence to the level of philosophical reflection, and assigns philosophy the fundamental task of settling the human question. Viewed differently—and if we include his *Philosophy of the Artistic Life*—by 1950 it was clear that Ramos deserved to be counted among the authors found in encyclopedias and histories. But he had to articulate philosophically the analysis of existence and develop the theory of the human being on rational grounds. *Toward a New Humanism* satisfies these criteria.

First, Ramos shares the supposition underwriting the various philosophical positions of the time: that the aim, in response to naturalism, was to restore authentically human values on positive grounds. Specifically, the grounds provided by the philosophies of Scheler, Hartmann, Heidegger, Ortega y Gasset, who provoked in Ramos an interest in the problem of the essence of the human being, thus helping to enrich the Mexican anthropological tradition.[5] Ramos also applies, in a new way, the philosophical axiom according to which *lo humano* constitutes a region of being; *lo humano*, he claims, "can only be considered from the ontology of existence." As a third point of departure, Ramos defines the human being as "an axiological entity," since an essential trait of human nature is the need for direction that gives life meaning and the need for purpose that justifies action.

The ontology of human existence developed by the Mexican philosopher restores the legitimate rights of instincts against spiritual dominance, and safeguards the higher forms of the soul against naturalism. Philosophy no longer makes the mistake of trying to explain nature from an anthropomorphic point of view or the mistake

---

5. This tradition was well underway before 1940. Compare to Oswaldo Robles, *Esquema de una antropología filosófica: Ensayo acerca las Relaciones entre el Espíritu y el Cuerpo* (Mexico: Editorial Pax, 1942). Although published after Ramos's *Toward a New Humanism*, Robles's *Esquema* is a developed version of his graduate thesis, published in 1935. There is historical evidence that Ramos was familiar with Robles's neo-Thomistic philosophical anthropology, and that Ramos's students at the National University were working on the subject at the time.

of understanding what it means to be human using the conceptual instruments of the sciences. The philosopher's job is only to explain each region of being using the categories discovered from within, not imported from without.

– IV –

This radical way of looking at things, which Samuel Ramos says implies a new conception of the human being, acknowledges all the facts that occur in human existence or that constitute it. It is not concerned with things, but with an objective order of realities and values that provide the "support and standard of human duties." Put differently, the facts are creations in which values reside, and the task of the philosopher is to present them to the axiological entity whole, and to put each value in its appropriate place, without overlooking the relations between or the dependencies on each axiological nucleus. The task of the philosopher, therefore, is to establish a hierarchical scale of values, one that provides reliable standards of action.

Samuel Ramos was clearly influenced by Nicolai Hartmann. The possibility of such a similar ontology is indebted to the modern theory of objects, according to which there are diverse layers of being, autonomous ontological regions, that produce the various disciplines. Each special science corresponds to a kind of being. Its principles are valid only when explaining its respective objects. Which means that singular interpretations of reality, such as naturalism, materialism, spiritualism, idealism, are partial and false, since they establish valuations and laws that are identical for all strata of being. There is no uniform system of laws in the universe; there are different types of law that belong to each order of being. This is why Samuel Ramos posits an ontological pluralism, a pluralism of the orders of being that, as a correlate, entails a pluralism of maximally general categories or principles as numerous as the "regional ontologies" of contemporary philosophy.

To develop the ontology of existence, Samuel Ramos applies the methods of phenomenology: to reveal "the essence of the human being *a priori*," that is, the set of characteristics that are inseparable from the idea of being human and that don't require empirical verification. Whether Ramos's reading of Husserl is accurate, the next step is to point out that the structural features obtained using this method are universally valid, and that individual and group variations fit into them. Since the phenomenological act is applied to an axiological *factum*, the Mexican philosopher claims that the essential features of the human being correspond to a historical period and to a singular existence, and that the features and forms of existence change according to the circumstances in which we find ourselves. In this way, the ontology of the axiological entity not only grounds the possibility of communication among human beings, but it also makes sense out of the thesis that each person does not lose their own character or modality. National and personal individualities remain unaffected. And just as in a single country the clash of different sensibilities produces a common soul, so it is, conversely, that the knowledge and realization of the same values create a human community.

The *Profile*, then, can be read as a philosophical anthropology of the Mexican. According to Ramos, there is an inherent law that makes the human being a process on the way to realization, an unfinished being realized in history. But history is singular. It is not surprising, then, that Ramos believes that both his analysis of the human being and of Mexican culture are philosophically valid. Furthermore, it is worth pointing out, and worth our closest attention, that the philosophical anthropology grounded in this ontology is not an abstraction or generalization. Strictly speaking, as Ramos liked to put it, it is a "conception of the concrete human."

– V –

The ontology of existence is the foundation or basis of humanism. Once the unity of the human being is established, not only is the path to humanizing culture open, but we will also have the standards to confront the disintegration of the human being that has produced today's many oppositions: between thought and life, the masculine and feminine, the masses and elites, the inferior and superior social classes, technology and science. This is the territory that defines the new humanism. It applies general and regional ontology to save us from the crisis of being human: from pure philosophical meditation to remedy, to studying what lies at the bottom of such woes, and to the solution to those woes. Values are its subject matter. And values provide the contours of an ideal type of human being, according to which one's behavior ought to be modeled. This humanism is *new* insofar as it is the result of a new way of conceiving of the human being, understood as a totality. Ramos claims that ontology captures the essence of being human under the category of a unity, "in the being of the totality," where particular elements are included and can be established. Physical, psychological, social, legal, and religious life are integrated into a whole without losing their individuality.

Like Scheler, Ramos sought the realization of the complete human being. This new humanism simultaneously makes possible the salvation of both the human being in general and the regional human being. It does not propose, as does Renaissance humanism, to lower the human from divine heights; philosophical reflection begins with the human historical *factum* and it ends by referring to the concrete human being. It signifies therefore an affirmation of the fact that human existence is constituted by two widely divergent values—the material and spiritual. The Mexican philosopher asserts, "The new humanism is more fully aware, much better informed, of the values peculiar to the human being and of their cosmic relations."

For Samuel Ramos, the evil of human beings, or what amounts to the same, of contemporary civilization, is produced by a poorly educated spirit. He is of the Socratic conviction that knowledge of oneself, achieved through an ontology of existence founded on reason, is how the lost equilibrium will be regained. "What modern humans lack is not the will to reform themselves, but the knowledge of the most reliable means to carry out this reform." To bring this new humanism into practice is the obligation of the philosopher, since in fact it is the responsibility of philosophy to construct with a sense of urgency "an ideological front to oppose the errors that undermine the very basis of human existence itself." In the end, the solution to the problems today depends on the new humanism. "Today humanism emerges as an ideal to combat the sub-humanity brought about by bourgeois capitalism and materialism."

BIBLIOGRAPHY

Texts Pertaining to Samuel Ramos
In English

Kubitz, O. A. "Humanism in Mexico." *Philosophy and Phenomenological Research* 2, no. 2 (December 1941): 211–18.

Merrim, Stephanie. *A Latin American Existentialist Ethos: Modern Mexican Literature and Philosophy*. Albany: State University of New York Press, 2023.

Paz, Octavio. *The Labyrinth of Solitude and Other Writings*. Translated by Lysander Kemp, Yara Milos, and Rachel Philips Belash. New York: Grove Press, 1985.

Ramos, Samuel. "The History of Philosophy in Mexico (1943)." Translated by Robert Eli Sanchez Jr. In *Mexican Philosophy in the 20th Century: Essential Readings*, edited by Carlos Alberto Sánchez and Robert Eli Sanchez Jr., 63–72. New York: Oxford University Press, 2017.

———. *Profile of Man and Culture in Mexico*. Translated by Peter G. Earle. Austin: University of Text Press, 1962.

———. "Twenty Years of Education in Mexico (1941)." Translated by Robert Eli Sanchez Jr. In *Mexican Philosophy in the 20th Century: Essential Readings*, edited by Carlos Alberto Sánchez and Robert Eli Sanchez Jr., 53–62. New York: Oxford University Press, 2017.

Romanell, Patrick. *Making of the Mexican Mind: A Study in Recent Mexican Thought*. Lincoln: University of Nebraska Press, 1952.

———. "Ortega in Mexico: A Tribute to Samuel Ramos." *Journal of the History of Ideas* 21, no. 4 (October–December 1960): 600–608.

———. "Samuel Ramos on the Philosophy of Mexican Culture: Ortega and Unamuno in Mexico." *The Latin American Research Association* 10, no. 3 (Autumn 1975): 81–101.

Sánchez, Carlos Alberto. "From Ortega y Gasset to Mexican Existentialism: Toward a Philosophical Conception of Chicano Identity." *Southwest Philosophical Studies* 25, no. 1 (2003): 49–61.

———. *Mexican Philosophy for the 21st Century: Relajo, Zozobra, and Other Frameworks for Understanding Our World.* London: Bloomsbury Academic, 2023.

Sanchez Jr., Robert Eli. "The Philosophy of Mexican Culture." In *Latin American and Latinx Philosophy*, edited by Robert Eli Sanchez Jr., 100–119. New York: Routledge, 2020.

Schmidt, Henry C. *The Roots of Lo Mexicano: Self and Society in Mexican Thought, 1900–1934.* College Station: Texas A&M University Press, 1978.

Stabb, Martin S. *In Quest of Identity: Patterns in the Spanish American Essay of Ideas, 1890–1960.* Chapel Hill: University of North Carolina Press, 1967.

Uranga, Emilio. *Analysis of Mexican Being.* Translated by Carlos Alberto Sánchez. London: Bloomsbury Academic, 2021.

Xirau, Joaquin. "*Hacia un nuevo Humanismo (Toward a New Humanism).*" Review of *Toward a New Humanism* by Samuel Ramos. *Philosophy and Phenomenological Research* 2, no. 4 (June 1942): 558–60.

Villegas, Abelardo. "The Problem of Truth." Translated by Carlos Alberto Sánchez. In *Mexican Philosophy in the 20th Century: Essential Readings*, edited by Carlos Alberto Sánchez and Robert Eli Sanchez Jr., 53–62. New York: Oxford University Press, 2017.

In Spanish

Arreola Cortes, Raúl. *Samuel Ramos: La pasión por la cultura.* Morelia: Centro de Estudios sobre la Cultura Nicolaíta, Universidad michoacana de San Nicolás de Hidalgo, 1997.

Frost, Elsa. "El tema de Samuel Ramos." *Diálogos: Artes, Letras, Ciencias humanas* 15, no. 6 (noviembre–diciembre, 1979): 46–47.

Hernández Luna, Juan. *Samuel Ramos: Su filosofar sobre lo mexicano.* México: Universidad Nacional Autónoma de México, 1956.

Hurtado, Guillermo. "Samuel Ramos, filósofo." *Cuadernos Americanos* 139, no. 1 (2012): 59–69.

Leidenberger, Georg. "Samuel Ramos: *La historia de la filosofía en México* (1943). In *México como problema: Esbozo de una historia intelectual*, editado por Carlos Illades and Rodolfo Suárez, 222–38. México: Siglo XXI, 2012.

Palacios, Adela, coord. *Nuestro Samuel Ramos: Homenaje*. México, 1960.

Ramos, Samuel. "Teatro: Pirandello." In *Obras Completas*, vol. 1, 260–62. México City: Universidad Nacional Autónoma de México, 1975.

Salazar Mallen, Rubén. *Samuel Ramos*. México: Cuadernos de Cultura Popular, Secretaría de Educación Pública, 1968.

Toscano Medina, Marco Antonio. *Una cultura derivada: el filosofar sobre México de Samuel Ramos*. Morelia: Universidad Michoacana de San Nicolás de Hidalgo, 2002.

Villegas, Abelardo. *La filosofía de lo mexicano*. México: Fondo de Cultura Económica, 1960.

Zea, Leopoldo. "Hacia un nuevo humanismo." *Tierra Nueva. Revista de Letras Universitarias* 1, no. 6 (nov.–dic., 1940): 374–78.

———. "Vasconcelos y Ramos en la filosofía mexicana." *Diánoia* 6, no. 6 (1960): 115–26.

Extended Bibliography

Bakewell, Sarah. *Humanly Possible: Seven Hundred Years of Humanist Freethinking, Inquiry, and Hope*. New York: Penguin Press, 2023.

Barrett, William. *Death of the Soul: From Descartes to the Computer*. Garden City: Anchor Books, 1986.

———. *The Illusion of Technique: A Search for Meaning in a Technological Civilization*. Garden City: Anchor Books, 1979.

Bergson, Henri. *Creative Evolution*. Translated by Arthur Mitchel. New York: Henry Holt and Company, 1911.

———. *Time and Free Will: An Essay on the Immediate Data of Consciousness*. Translated by F. L. Pogson. London: George Allen & Unwin, 1953.

Boutroux, Émile. *The Contingency of the Laws of Nature*. Translated by Fred Rothwell. Chicago and London: Open Court Publishing Company, 1916.

Bowler, Peter. *Charles Darwin: The Man and His Influence.* London: Blackwell Publishers, 1990.

Büchner, Ludwig. *Force and Matter: Empirico-Philosophical Studies Intelligibly Rendered.* London: Trübner & Co, 1870.

Descartes, René. *Meditations on First Philosophy: With Selections from the Objections and Replies.* Translated by Michael Moriarty. Oxford: Oxford University Press, 2008.

———. "Treatise on Man." In *The World and Other Writings*, 97–169. Cambridge: Cambridge University Press, 1998.

Epicurus. "Letter to Menoeceus." In *Principle Doctrines*, translated by Russel Greer. Library of Liberal Arts, 1978.

Fichte, Johann Gottlieb. *The Vocation of Man.* Translated by Peter Preuss. Indianapolis: Hackett Publishing Company, 1987.

———. "The Vocation of Man." In *Works*, translated by William Smith. Perfect Library, 2013.

García Morente, Manuel. *Ensayos sobre el progreso.* Madrid: Ediciones Encuentro, 1932.

Gerchenson, M. O. and V. I. Ivanov. "A Correspondence Between Two Corners." Translated by Norbert Guterman. *Parisian Review* 9 (September 1948): 951–1048.

Haddox, John H. *Antonio Caso: Philosopher of Mexico.* Austin: University of Texas Press, 1971.

———. *Vasconcelos of Mexico: Philosopher and Prophet.* Austin: University of Texas Press, 1967.

Haeckel, Ernst. *Monism as Connecting Religion and Science: The Confession of Faith of a Man of Science.* London: Adam and Charles Black, 1895.

Hartmann, Nicolai. *Der Aufbau der realen Welt. Grundriss der allgemeinen Kategorienlehre.* Berlin: De Gruyter, 1940.

———. *Ethics*, 3 Volumes. Translated by Stanton Coit. London: George Allen & Unwin, 1932.

———. *Possibility and Actuality.* Translated by Stephanie Adair and Alex Scott. Berlin: De Gruyter, 2013.

Hook, Sidney. *Towards the Understanding of Karl Marx: A Revolutionary Interpretation.* London: Victor Gollancz, 1933.

Hurtado, Guillermo. "El pensamiento ante la guerra mundial." *La Razón de México*, March 30, 2024. https://www.razon.com.mx/opinion/columnas/guillermo-hurtado/pensamiento-mexicano-guerra-mundial-570993.

Klages, Ludwig. *Der Geist als Widersacher der Seele*. Leipzig: Johan Ambrosius Barth, 1929.

———. *The Science of Character*. Translated by W. H. Johnston. London: George Allen & Unwin, 1929.

Lamiell, James T. *William Stern (1871–1938): A Brief Introduction to His Life and Works*. Lengerich: Papst Science Publishers, 2010.

Nietzsche, Friedrich. *Genealogy of Morals*. Edited by Keith Ansell Pearson. Translated by Carol Diethe. Cambridge: Cambridge University Press, 2007.

Ortega y Gasset, José. "Introduction to an Estimative Science: What Are Values." Translated by Carlos Alberto Sánchez. In *The New Yearbook of Phenomenology and Phenomenological Philosophy: Special Issue: Phenomenology in the Hispanic World*, edited by Antonio Zirión Quijano, Jethro Bravo González, Noé Expósito Ropero, and Jonathan Jehu Guereca Carreón, 125–39. New York: Routledge, 2023.

———. "Max Scheler, un embriagado de esencias." In *Obras Completas*, vol. 4. Madrid: Revista de Occidente, 1966.

———. *Meditations on Quixote*. Translated by Evelyn Rugg and Diego Marín. Urbana and Chicago: University of Illinois Press, 1961.

———. *Mission of the University*. Translated by Howard Lee Nostrand. New York: Routledge, 1946.

———. *The Modern Theme*. Translated by Lames Cleugh. New York: Harper Torchbooks, 1961.

———. "Vitalidad, alma, espíritu." In *Obras Completas*, vol. 2: El Espectador (1916–1934). Madrid: *Revista de Occidente*, 1963.

———. *What Is Philosophy?* Translated by Mildred Adams. New York: Norton Library, 1960.

Robles, Oswaldo. *Esquema de una antropología filosófica: Ensayo acerca las relaciones entre el Espíritu y el Cuerpo*. Mexico: Editorial Pax, 1942.

Rousseau, Jean-Jacques. *The Social Contract & Discourses*. Translated by G. D. H. Cole. London and Toronto: J. M. Dent & Sons, 1913.

Sánchez Villaseñor, José. *Ortega y Gasset, Existentialist: A Critical Study of His Thought and Its Sources*. Translated by Joseph Small, S. J. Chicago: Henry Regnery Company, 1949.

Scheler, Max. *Formalism in Ethics and Non-Formal Ethics of Values*. Translated by Manfred S. Frings and Roger L. Funk. Evanston, IL: Northwestern University Press, 1973.

———. "The Forms of Knowledge and Culture." In *Philosophical Perspectives*, translated by Oscar Haac. Boston: Beacon Press, 1958.

———. *The Human Place in the Cosmos*. Translated by Manfred Frings. Evanston, IL: Northwestern University Press, 2009.

———. "Love and Knowledge." In *On Feeling, Knowing, and Value: Selected Writings*, translated by H. J. Bershady with assistance of P. Haley. Chicago and London: The University of Chicago Press, 1992.

———. "Man and History." In *Philosophical Perspectives*, translated by Oscar Haac. Boston: Beacon Press, 1958.

———. *The Nature of Sympathy*. Translated by Peter Heath Hamden. London: Routledge and Kegan Press, 1954.

———. *Ressentiment*. Translated by Louis A. Coser. Milwaukee: Marquette University Press, 1998.

Simmel, Georg. "The Concept and Tragedy of Culture." In *Simmel on Culture: Selected Writings*, edited by David Frisby and Mike Featherstone, translated by Mark Ritter and David Frisby. London: Sage, 1997.

Soldatenko, Michael. "Perspectivist Chicano Studies, 1970–1985." *Ethnic Studies Review* 19, no. 2–3 (June/October 1996): 181–208.

Sombart, Werner. *The Quintessence of Capitalism: The Study of the History and Psychology of the Modern Business Man*. Translated by M. Epstein. New York: E. P. Dutton and Company, 1915.

Unamuno, Miguel de. "Civilización y cultura." In *Obras Selectas*, 153–59. Madrid: Biblioteca Nueva, 1986.

Vasconcelos, José. "Books I Read Sitting and Books I Read Standing." In *the Modern Mexican Essay*, edited by José Luis Martínez, translated by H. W. Hilborn, 97–100. Toronto: University of Toronto Press, 1975.

Windelband, Wilhelm. *Logic*. Translated by B. E. Meyer. London: Macmillan, 1913.

INDEX

anarchy, 51, 93, 102
Aristotle, 3, 21n3, 40, 41, 47, 135
art, xii, 9
    artistic, 51, 54, 79, 102, 146
automaton, 11, 68, 114
axiology xx, 39, 56, 67–69, 79, 146–48

beauty, 40, 51, 80, 99
Bergson, Henri, 6, 12, 25, 30–34, 41, 44, 65, 89, 126, 132–33, 153
biology, 29, 44, 47, 88, 135
bourgeoisie, xviii, xxi, 2–3, 6, 15–16, 149
Boutroux, Émile, 31, 34, 45, 69, 70n5, 133
Büchner, Ludwig, 6

capitalism, xviii, 3n2, 15–16, 149
Caso, Antonio, xi, 144
categorical imperative, 59, 81
chauffeur, 108
Christianity, 2, 40–42, 63, 66, 122
civilization
    and economics, 90
    as instrument of death, 87
    as instrument of freedom, 72
    positive meaning of, 87, 89, 108–10
    taking advantage of natural forces, 67
    technical civilization, xix, 109
    transformation of nature, 57
    what it has denied humanity, 11
community, 64, 83, 85, 120, 132, 148
cosmos, xx, 34, 65, 72n7, 117
culture
    as the Beautiful, the Good, the True, 51, 80
    as consciousness of values, 55–56
    correct account of values, 61
    as humanization, 38, 102
    and objectivity, 52
    spiritual sense of life, 2
    transformation of nature, 57
    as a universal vision of things, 61

Darwin, Charles, 6, 88–89
Dasein, 132–55
Descartes, René, xviii–xix, 3–4, 21–23, 32, 35, 47, 57, 126, 130n3
destiny, xi–xiii, 13, 16–17, 26, 37, 39, 87–88, 99–103, 113, 126, 128
determinism, 6, 66–71, 89
dictator(ship), 93, 107

Dilthey, Wilhelm, 6, 21, 26, 44, 78
dualism, xviii–xix, 1–4, 13, 47, 69, 94, 125, 141

economics, 1, 8, 15, 41, 44, 79
Epicurus, 122
epiphenomenon, 36, 44
epoch, 24, 26, 51, 118, 121
ethos, 78, 98
eticidad, 81
existentialism, xivn8, 21n3, 21–25, 31, 121, 131–33

Feuerbach, Ludwig, 6
Fichte, Johann Gottlieb, 63–64, 81
finalism, 48, 57, 67, 71
Freud, Sigmund, 41, 121

Galileo, 3
García Morente, Manuel, 20–21, 28n9, 31–32, 56, 63n5, 122
geometric, 25–26, 30
Greek, 2, 13, 33, 40–42, 47, 77, 81, 141

Haeckel, Ernst, 6
Hegel, Georg Wilhelm Friedrich, 41, 135
Heidegger, Martin, 21, 31, 34–36, 121, 131–35, 146
Hobbes, Thomas, 6, 41
homo faber, 41
homo mensura, 51

Husserl, Edmund, xxi, 27–34, 119–20, 130–35, 148

idealism
    antithesis of realism, 32
    form of subjectivism, xx, 21, 59, 91
    Plato's form of, 57
infrahuman, 42
instinct, 2, 5–6, 41, 43–44, 48, 83, 93
intuition, v, 18, 22, 27–30, 34
irrational, 66, 92, 93, 113, 145
    irrationalism, xxv, 93

Jesus, 56
justice, xiii, 16, 55, 100

Kant, Immanuel, xii, xxi, 21, 25–26, 41, 56–57, 59, 62–63, 66–67, 100, 130–31
Kierkegaard, Søren, xviin12, 7, 109n5
Klages, Ludwig, 8, 42, 75–76
knowledge
    accumulation of, xvii, xxiv, 27, 56
    knowledge-relation, 20–22
    philosophical knowledge, 67
    technical side of, xviii, 27, 93

La Mettrie, Julian Offray de, 5
Leibniz, 4, 69
liberty, 11, 13, 38, 108–9, 125
logos, 22, 41, 118

machinism, 5n5
    See mechanism
Malebranche, 4
Marx, Karl, 15n21, 41
Marxism, 15n21, 90
mask, 11, 75–76
materialism, xi–xii, xviii, xx, 3, 5,
    65, 94, 114, 147, 149
    historical, xi–xii, xviii, xxv,
    90, 137
mechanism, 5, 43, 48, 57, 65, 69,
    106–8
mechanization, xxiii, 5n5, 106–10
Messer, August, 64
Mexico, 52, 61n1, 106, 112–16
modern
    civilization, 112, 114
    humans, 3, 8–12, 53, 107
    life, 107
    Mexico, xii
    modernity, 111, 47, 77
    philosophy, xxi, xxvi, 21n3,
    40, 65, 137–38, 146
monism, 6, 67

naturalism, xviii, 91, 132, 146–47
    naturalist, xxi, 6, 44, 81, 91,
    94
Nietzsche, Friedrich, 1, 6–8, 41,
    44, 111

objectivity, 49–50, 144
    of values, xxi, 51–58
ontic, 30, 36, 132
ontological, 4, 22–23, 29–31, 36,
    40, 47, 79, 132, 145, 147

regional ontology, xxi, 31,
    45, 147, 149
originality, xxii, 84, 91, 136, 143
Ortega y Gasset, José, 7–9,
    30–32, 48–50, 115–19,
    124–29
    Revista de Occidente, 7n7,
    9n11, 28n9, 48n6, 53, 98,
    119
overproduction, 10

person
    forming world of one's own,
    78
    highest goal of humanization,
    75
    lack of in Mexico, 103
    the true self, 77
phenomenology, 28, 34–35,
    130–33, 147
physiognomy, 24, 75, 78
Pirandello, 13
Plato, 5, 47, 56, 57, 94, 122, 126
Platonism, 55
politics, 93, 103
    human being as political
    animal, 38, 133
    political regimes, 114
    See also anarchy
positivism, xi, xviii, 5, 65, 141
power, 5, 8–9, 25, 41, 44, 48,
    57, 60, 68, 72–73, 78–87, 89,
    92–93, 106, 114, 137
*Profile of Man and Culture in
    Mexico*, 61n1, 75, 111, 113n4,
    128, 137–38, 144, 148

Protagoras, 53
psychoanalysis, 113
psychology, 12, 29, 47, 51–52, 101, 113, 121, 135
   bourgeois, xviii, 2, 6

realism, 22, 96, 130–32
   antithesis to idealism, xx, 20, 21n3, 31
relativism, 24
religion, 17, 41, 122, 125
Renaissance, xx, 42, 75, 81, 111–12, 116, 120, 149
Romanticism, 59, 81, 92
Rousseau, Jean-Jacques, 7

salvation, 17, 104, 113, 137, 139–40, 144, 149
Scheler, Max, 31, 24, 39–42, 50, 53–54, 63, 72, 79–80, 83–84, 94, 98–105, 119–21, 126, 130–37, 141, 146, 149
Scholastic, 3, 68
self, 12–14, 49, 77, 84
Simmel, Georg, 9–10
skepticism, 52
sociology, 29, 91, 131
Socratic, xiii, 88, 145, 149
Sombart, Werner, 2–3, 15
Spengler, Oswald, xviii, 1, 8, 42, 119, 126
Spinoza, 4, 70
spirit
   as capacity to make oneself object of value, 40
   as center of person, 49
   spiritualism, xviii, xx, 5, 92, 94, 147
Spranger, Eduard, 62n3, 79, 80n3, 132
subhumanity, 16, 112
subjective, 50, 52–54, 59, 61, 77, 79, 82, 85, 91
subjectivism, xx, 21, 51–54, 59, 91
superstructure, 90

technology, xiii, xix, xxiv, 8, 101, 142, 148
   fever for, 10
teleological, 37, 40, 57, 67–68

values
   table of, xviii, 51, 72–73
Vasconcelos, José, xi, xxiv, 98, 104, 140, 144
vital, 92–93, 142
   circumstance, 24
   experience, 20, 96, 141
   impulse, 38, 89
   interest, 90
   organs, 107
   problems, 88, 125
   reason, 28, 132
   vitality, 48–50, 94, 113, 133
vocation, 11, 64, 81, 145
   of being human, 63

Windelband, Wilhelm, 19, 32
wisdom, 61, 72, 113, 140–41